Shadows
of Doubt

D0892959

Shadows
of Doubt

Noel Redican

MERCIER PRESS
WHAT YOU NEED TO READ

MERCIER PRESS

Cork

www.mercierpress.ie

Trade enquiries to CMD Distribution
55A Spruce Avenue, Stillorgan Industrial Park,
Blackrock, County Dublin

© Noel Redican, 2008
ISBN: 978 1 85635 594 0

10 9 8 7 6 5 4 3 2 1

A CIP record for this title is available from the British Library

Dedicated to my dear wife, Teresa, for her patience and tolerance of my
ever changing moods over the six years it took me to finish this work. God
rest you, John Hughes, Seán Farrell and Dinny Fitz.

Mercier Press receives financial assistance from the
Arts Council/An Chomhairle Ealaíon

*This book is sold subject to the condition that it shall not, by way of trade or otherwise, be
lent, resold, hired out or otherwise circulated without the publisher's prior consent in any
form of binding or cover other than that in which it is published and without a similar
condition including this condition being imposed on the subsequent purchaser.*

*No part of this publication may be reproduced or transmitted in any form or by any means,
electronic or mechanical, including photocopying, recording or any information or retrieval
system, without the prior permission of the publisher in writing.*

Printed and bound in the EU

Contents

Introduction   7

Chapter *1*

The Killing of Timothy Coughlan   11

Chapter *2*

Collins' Man: According to Seán Harling   20

Chapter *3*

De Valera's Man: According to Seán Harling   33

Chapter *4*

The Redicans   51

Chapter *5*

Fianna Éireann   60

Chapter *6*

The Redicans Continued   74

Chapter *7*

De Valera's Quest for Power   91

Chapter *8*

From Heroes to Rogues   113

Chapter *9*

The Attack   126

Chapter *10*

The Tribunal of Inquiry   139

Chapter *11*

Pining for His Family   163

Chapter *12*

Power at Last for de Valera   171

Chapter *13*

Cosy Little Chats   190

Epilogue   213

Acknowledgements   222

Introduction

Those who blindly followed leaders who had themselves gone wrong become traitors to the republic and deserve a traitor's fate.

Fianna Éireann constitution

The above is a quotation from the constitution of a militant Irish republican boy-scout organisation, Fianna Éireann. But it also held true for all militant Irish republican organisations right up until the late 1940s.

When Éamon de Valera, the last leader of the 1916 rising to surrender and the only one to dodge the firing squad, was released from prison on 16 June 1917, he became the runaway winner of a by-election in east Clare for Sinn Féin and was elected president of the party. Then, at their *ardfheis* in October 1917, Sinn Féin unanimously adopted two significant and fundamental policies: the refusal to take seats in the British House of Commons and the amendment of their constitution to declare that a republic was the aim of their organisation. Furthermore, all who joined the republican movement were required to swear an oath of allegiance to the Irish republic. This, I believe, is where the republican idea of 'going wrong' really stems from, although it could well be argued that John Redmond and the 170,000 men who followed him back in 1914 were the first to 'go wrong' when they split from the republican Irish Volunteers movement to back Britain in the First World War.

The taking of this oath was an integral part of the militant republican ethos. Any man who had sworn allegiance to the republic and then decided to swear allegiance to a non-republican organisation (a lesser authority) was branded a traitor. Many an unfortunate man who was thus branded was found either at the back of a dark alleyway or on some lonely foothill with a bullet through the back of his head, as retribution for 'going wrong'.

In the general election of December 1918 Sinn Féin won seventy-three seats out of a hundred and five, having held only seven going in. They now had, they believed, the full backing of the majority of the Irish people for their policy of abstentionism, but better still, they believed they had the people's consent to go to war with the British army to win the right to set up a free and independent Irish republic.

On 21 January 1919 Sinn Féin set up the first Dáil Éireann in the Mansion House, Dublin. Éamon de Valera, who was in Lincoln prison at the time, was elected president, Michael Collins minister for finance and Cathal Brugha minister for defence. They waged a guerrilla war against the British army which eventually caused the British government to negotiate a peace Treaty and brought the republican movement to a bitter split. Michael Collins, Arthur Griffith and Richard Mulcahy accepted the terms of the Treaty but Éamon de Valera, Cathal Brugha and Austin Stack rejected them. The latter accused the former of betrayal and of 'going wrong'.

On 10 January 1922, after signing allegiance to the British crown, Collins, Griffith and Mulcahy set up what the anti-Treaty republicans claimed was a puppet government for the British in the Mansion House, Dublin. They later moved to Leinster House, a building that de Valera and his followers swore they would never set foot in until a thirty-two-county Irish republic was established. Then, at 4 a.m. on Wednesday 28 June 1922, a bloody and savage civil war began for control of the country between the defenders of the republic and those who had 'gone wrong'.

The story told in this work is based on fact and hearsay about a high-ranking officer in Fianna Éireann who, after eleven years of being a staunch republican activist, finally joined the Free State secret service (more commonly known as the Specials) in 1926. His name was Seán Harling, commanding officer of the Dublin Brigade of Fianna Éireann and chauffeur to Constance, Countess Markievicz – Fianna Éireann's commander-in-chief and founder – and the man chosen by the republican hierarchy to organise and take charge of the policing of the first Dáil sitting and those that followed.

But Harling wasn't the first or the last to 'go wrong' according to republican ethos, for in 1927, four years after the civil war ended, anti-Treaty republicans led by Éamon de Valera entered Leinster House without having achieved their declared aim of an Irish republic. During the election campaign of September 1927, W. T. Cosgrave's Cumann na nGaedheal placed a slogan in the papers reminding the electorate of how Fianna Fáil came to be in Leinster House: 'They took the oath to save their Party: They would not take it to save the country from Civil War.'

So in the end the entire republican movement, except of course Austin Stack's Sinn Féin and Seán Russell's IRA, 'went wrong'. Whether those who 'went wrong' were right or wrong to do so is not for debate in this work. It is according to republican ethos that they 'went wrong', and it is purely from the perspective of that idea that this book is written.

Chapter 1

The Killing of Timothy Coughlan

At exactly 6.15 p.m. on Saturday, 28 January 1928, an official garda car pulled up at the kerb outside Pearse Street garda station. The driver, Garda James Whelan, had been ordered by his boss, Superintendent Finian O'Driscoll, who was a pedant for punctuality, to be there at precisely that time to take him home to tea. He was taking a half-hour break.

As he was going out the door, O'Driscoll bumped into one of his subordinates, Special Intelligence Officer Seán Harling, who had just finished his shift and was going home. O'Driscoll offered him a lift as far as Kenilworth Square. Harling accepted the lift, even though it would mean a twenty-minute walk to his house. The tram would have left him almost on his doorstep.

It had been a long, boring day for the two men and neither spoke a word for the whole of the journey. Harling was dropped off at the corner of Kenilworth Square beside the Rathgar catholic church at about 6.25 p.m. He bid O'Driscoll and Whelan goodnight and the car drove off to 50 Kenilworth Square, O'Driscoll's house.

It was a cold, bleak January night. Harling pulled the brim of his hat down over his forehead so that it was touching the rim of his black horn-rimmed glasses. He pulled the thick collar of his heavy winter overcoat up around his neck, pushed his woollen gloves tightly onto his hands, then walked briskly along Frankford Avenue towards Woodpark lodge, where he, his wife and baby daughter lived with his in-laws, the Redicans.

At home in that humble abode was Thomas Redican senior, who was sitting at the table in the tiny kitchen reading the evening paper. James (Jim), the eldest of the Redican siblings, an ex-IRA activist and convicted bank robber, now unemployed, and Laurence (Larry), the youngest in the family and an apprentice mechanic, were sitting on one side of the range studying form for the next day's horse racing. Seated on the other side of the range was their only sister, Dorothy (Nora), Harling's wife, keeping a watchful eye on her seventeen-month-old daughter Nancy, who was playing close to the fire. Chatting over by the tiny kitchen window were the mother, Anne, and her second eldest, Thomas (Tom) junior, a private in the Free State army. Tom had only arrived home at three o'clock that afternoon on leave from the Curragh, where he was stationed, and was still in uniform. Like his older brother, Tom was also an ex-republican activist and convicted bank robber. The other brother, Patrick (Paddy), an apprentice butcher, had not yet come home from work.

Harling reached the Dartry Road at 6.35 p.m., walking on the left-hand side, the dark side. When he reached Temple Road he spotted two unsavoury-looking characters sitting on a seat under the shadow of overhanging trees on the far side of the road, near St Kevin's Park and in front of a house called Ard-na-Cree. 'Who the hell are those two over there? And what are they up to?' he wondered.

When the two men saw him approaching they stood up, took a good look over, then walked slowly ahead of him towards the tramway terminus, the direction he was going. He noticed that one was slightly taller than the other and was wearing a fawnish-brown trenchcoat. The other wore a black cloth overcoat. They periodically glanced back at him as though making sure he was still there. Feeling nervous and exposed, Harling continued walking at his brisk pace, keeping his eyes focused on the two men. Halfway between Temple Road and Woodpark lodge he drew abreast of them and threw a piercing glance over as he moved marginally ahead.

He had every reason to be afraid, for he knew that Fianna Fáil/IRA had ordered his execution for spying on them for the state. 'Those two are surely here to do me,' he thought and, anticipating an attack, took cover behind a tram standard, only yards from his home, praying that the two men would keep walking.

He pulled the woollen mitten off his right hand and patted his cold .45 Webley automatic gently, as though patting a loyal comrade on the back in gratitude for being there to help defend his life on that cold, dark and lonely Dartry Road against the men sent out to kill him.

A woman passed by the standard but he hardly noticed her. He was too concerned about getting home safely to his wife and child to take his eyes off the two shady-looking characters across the road, who had stopped after seeing their target take cover.

After about a minute he decided to make a run for it. Clutching his trusty .45 firmly, he darted the remaining few yards to the lodge. But just as he reached the gates, going down on bended knee, they opened fire, narrowly missing him. He let off a round at the two men, who were now running across the road towards him. He dived into the lodge porch as they fired four more shots. Reaching the porch safely, he crouched behind a tiny wall and pillar for cover.

The area around Woodpark lodge was in total darkness save for the hint of light peeping out from behind the curtain that hung on the tiny kitchen window. He peered nervously into the darkness, listening intently for the slightest sound that would reveal the whereabouts of his attackers. He heard footsteps. Then out of the darkness came two more shots. The flashes blinded him momentarily. A bullet took a chip out of the pillar he was crouching behind and whizzed barely half an inch past his ear before lodging in the door behind him.

Then a blurry shape loomed only feet in front of him. He fired once at the figure, then reached behind with his left hand, feeling for the doorknob but keeping his eyes fixed on the darkness in front of him and his gun at the ready. He opened the door and backed into the narrow hallway, not knowing whether he had hit the blurry figure outside. And as he was closing the door, he heard the sound of footsteps running away.

Harling's young daughter had the habit of toddling out to the hallway to meet her father when she heard him coming in from work. Mindful of this as he backed up to the kitchen door, he called out, 'Nora, mind the baby! The house is under attack. Someone come and bolt the door!'

Nora ran to her baby. Harling's brother-in-law, Tom, ran to bolt the door and heard groaning from without.

'I think there's someone hit outside, Seán,' he told Harling.

'Step back from the door, Tom,' Harling ordered. 'It might be a trick to get me outside.'

Harling went to enter the kitchen, but as soon as his figure appeared at the door James, who was standing ready for action, threw a bucket of water at him, thinking he was an intruder. Harling, wet all over, cursed and grumbled but quickly got over it.

For the next five minutes they stood silently on guard in the tiny kitchen, listening for the sound of intruders and ready to defend themselves and their home from attack. But no attack came.

Harling broke the silence, saying, 'Come on, Tom, I think it's time we checked outside.'

Tom unbolted the door and slowly opened it while Harling covered him. They peered into the darkness and saw the figure of a man lying on the ground about four feet away from the porch pillar where Harling had earlier taken cover. Harling cried out several times, 'Are you wounded? Are you hit?'

There was no reply. Redican went to the man, while Harling kept him covered, and asked, 'My poor man, where did you get hit up?'

The man just grunted.

'Check to see if he is armed, Tom,' Harling ordered.

Redican searched around the body and found a gun on the ground only inches from the man's right hand. He handed it to Harling, who put it in the breast pocket of his coat, then ordered Redican to run down to Rathmines police station and alert the guards to what had taken place.

Harling went to the body to see if he recognised his attacker, but he did not. He then called James out to help him carry the dying man into the house. They laid him on the kitchen floor near the door, his feet facing the hallway and his head facing the fireplace. When Harling went out to bolt the door James noticed the remnant of a cigarette between the dying man's lips and tried to extract it to give him more air, but he only managed to knock the ash out. The paper stuck to the man's lips.

The two men were standing watch in the hallway when a knock came to the door.

'Who's there?' shouted Harling.

'A messenger from the Home and Colonial with parcels.

'Leave them there on the wall,' ordered Redican.

About four or five minutes later there came another knock.

'Who is it?' asked Harling.

'A policeman on duty from Rathmines,' replied a voice.

'Are you in uniform?' Harling asked.

'Yes,' the voice replied.

'Then go to the window to see if we can recognise you,' ordered Harling.

He went to the window and Redican recognised him as being from Rathmines. They let him in and, having filled him in, Special Intelligence Officer Seán Harling told him to go and fetch the priest and to ring up the Detective Branch at Pearse Street.

A short time later another knock came, accompanied by a voice saying, 'Police! Open up!'

'Are you in uniform?' yelled Harling.

'No,' was the reply.

'I can't let you in unless I can identify you,' Harling told him.

'You'll recognise me all right. I am from Rathmines,' shouted the man.

'Go to the window,' ordered Harling.

He went to the window and Redican recognised him as a Detective McWilliams, a north of Ireland man stationed at Rathmines. He was admitted. Harling explained what had happened, then sent him off to summon aid.

Shortly after McWilliams left, a priest arrived, but he was not the one they had sent for. This priest was a complete stranger to them. He did not utter a word as he came through the door but went straight to the dying man, knelt down beside him and whispered into his ear. And when Harling told him that he had earlier knelt beside the man and said an act of contrition, the priest did not acknowledge him. Instead, he suddenly stood up, made the sign of the cross over the body, and with bent head hurriedly left the house without having uttered a single word. They never found out who he was, which parish he had come from or who had informed him about the incident.

Soon a group of detective officers arrived from Pearse Street, Officer Coogan being one of them. Then came Fr Hurley, the priest sent for. He administered the last sacraments to the dying man and went on his way.

As soon as Fr Hurley had closed the door behind him, Special Intelligence Officers Coogan and Harling searched the dying man's person for clues to his identity. Harling found a Fianna Fáil membership card in the breast pocket of the victim's coat with 'Timothy Coughlan, 24 Ring Street, Inchicore' written inside. He recognised the name and remembered having heard about Coughlan and having seen him once at a Fianna Éireann *aeridh-eacht* (open-air convention) in Shelbourne Park back in May 1922, when he had been commandant in the Second Battalion, Dublin Brigade, and Coughlan had been in the Fourth. He had never met him since.

Coogan and Harling had just finished searching the victim when Superintendents O'Driscoll and Ennis and a crowd of other policemen arrived. Harling explained to O'Driscoll, his immediate superior, what had taken place, then handed the .38 automatic pistol found beside Coughlan's body over to O'Driscoll and his own weapon to Ennis. The detective superintendents examined the weapons carefully. Harling's was found to contain two spent and four live cartridges. A Webley retains spent cartridges whereas a .38 Colt ejects them after firing. Coughlan's gun was empty. A little later, an ambulance from the Army Medical Corps arrived and took the wounded Coughlan to the Meath hospital.

Seán Harling, backed up by the Redicans, told the jury of

ten men in the coroner's court at the inquest held at the Meath hospital, Dublin on 30 January 1928 that that was the truth of what happened to Timothy Coughlan on that fateful night. The commissioner of police and the Department of Justice readily accepted his explanation.

But the jury, when they had analysed the evidence presented to the inquest by Wilfred Francis Lane, MB, who had been on duty in the Meath hospital the night Coughlan was brought in, did not accept it. Lane told the inquest that Coughlan was dead on admission.

'The death in my opinion had occurred a short time previously,' Lane testified. 'By order of the coroner, Dr Louis Byrne, I did a post-mortem examination and found that there were two wounds, one at the back of the head, the other on the forehead, both on the left-hand side. There were three lines of fracture extending from this wound. The track of the missile plainly connected in a straight line the entrance and exit wounds.

'I am of the opinion that the wound at the back of the head was the entrance wound of the missile, the wound on the forehead the exit wound. I would say he was shot from behind at close quarters. In the general examination of the body I found the right hand partially clenched and between the lips were the remnants of a cigarette. Death in my opinion was due to shock, haemorrhage and laceration of the brain.'

In answer to a question from the coroner, Lane replied, 'It was the one bullet caused the injuries. There was no other wound. The bullet was travelling rapidly and with great force at the time.'

Answering a question from Mr O'Connor, KC, for the next of kin, he said, 'All the injuries were caused by the one bullet except possibly an independent fracture about two inches above the temple on the left side of the head, which could have been caused by a fall. It would want to have been a severe fall. It might have been caused by violence, by sandbag for instance.'

The jury, who swore that they would true verdict give, without fear, favour, affection or ill-will, according to the evidence laid before them, returned their verdict: 'We find that the said Timothy Coughlan died on twenty-eighth instant from shock, haemorrhage and laceration of the brain caused by a bullet.' But, much to the annoyance of the Detective Branch at Pearse Street and the Department of Justice, they added a rider: 'We are of the opinion that the circumstances of the case should be a matter of further investigation.'

Chapter 2

Collins' Man:
According to Seán Harling

Seán Harling was born in Dublin on 21 May 1902 and reared at 20 Phibsborough Road, adjacent to the Great Western and Midland Railway in Broadstone where all his family and relations worked. He attended Brunswick Street primary school, where he excelled in history and was regularly praised by the teachers for his ability to remember historical events and dates. His father, mother, family and relations were staunch Larkinites and labour politics was a regular topic around the Harling kitchen table. Meetings between 'Big Jim' Larkin and shop stewards from the railway were nearly always held in the Harling home.

Seán loved to tell of how he first met Big Jim in the flesh.

'It was early one Friday evening. I wasn't long in from school when I heard this thunderous knock on the front door that frightened the life out of me. My father answered the door. I heard loud greetings, then in walked Big Jim, and he said to me, "Can I have a loan of that chair, son?"

'"Course you can, Mr Larkin."

'"How do you know me?" he asked.

'"I seen you speaking in O'Connell Street," I answered while handing him the chair.

'He used the chair to stand on when he addressed the railwaymen coming out of work just outside our hall door.'

Seán did not show much interest in the labour movement,

but from a very early age he developed a keen interest in Irish nationalism. Shortly after his thirteenth birthday in 1915, he and his pal, Bobby Tweedale, joined the North Dublin City District Unit of Fianna Éireann, which was under the command of Lieutenant Prendergast. Seán Heuston, who was executed by the British in 1916 for being one of the leaders of the rising, was officer commanding of the North Dublin District. Con Colbert, who was also executed in 1916, was OC of the South Dublin District.

Harling said of the initiation ceremony that 'What impressed us most was the tall young woman on the platform exhorting us to be loyal and true to Ireland and to learn to defend our country's right to become a free and independent nation by force of arms if necessary. That young woman was the Countess Markievicz.' The boys had to buy their own uniforms and had their green shirts made by their mothers or some good neighbour who was handy with a needle.

Countess Markievicz set up the Fianna with Bulmer Hobson, a leader in the secretive Irish Republican Brotherhood, in response to Baden Powell setting up the boy scouts in Lord Iveagh's grounds off Harcourt Street, Dublin. The sole purpose of the boy scouts, as the republican movement saw it, was to recruit young Irish boys to be trained as soldiers and eventually to become cannon fodder for the British army.

Fianna Éireann was a strict militant republican boy-scout organisation and taught its young members the sad political history of Ireland. The boys did physical training, were taught Morse code and carried dispatches to and from volunteer branches around the city. They also participated in military drilling and revolver practice twice a week. Harling did his in the Hardwick hall in Hardwick Street, Dublin.

The first serious encounter Harling had with the crown forces was the morning he was sent out to Howth with some other Fianna boys to help unload the *Asgard*. They had with them a special type of handcart, called a trek-cart, which had a canvas cover and a long centre shaft. They filled the cart with rifles and ammunition and headed for town, but were confronted by a detachment of Scottish Borderers who had sealed off the bottom of the Clontarf Road. They quickly turned and made for Coolock village, pursued by some of the soldiers. Harling recalled, 'We hid in Reddin's fields until the Brits were gone and then we buried the cart, rifles and ammo there. They were dug up later by the Irish Volunteers and used in the rising.'

Those German Mausers became affectionately known as the Howth guns:

> How glorious was your feel,
> O, my old Howth gun!
> When you made the Saxon reel,
> O, my old Howth gun!
> When the Lancers trim and neat,
> Charging down O'Connell Street,
> Had to beat a quick retreat
> O, my old Howth gun!

My Old Howth Gun by Seamus McGallogly

At the beginning of the rising, Harling, Bobby Tweedale, Seán Howard and Howard's brother reported for duty to the volunteer post at the North Dublin Union in Brunswick Street. While helping to build a barricade there, Harling and his boys commandeered a coach from a coachbuilder's yard close by and used it as a makeshift door into the barricade. They carried dispatches to other nearby posts and kept the snipers on the roof supplied with bullets.

On the Wednesday the OC, Paddy Houlihan, gave a dispatch to Seán Howard to deliver to Captain Piaras Béaslaí down at the Fr Matthew hall in Church Street. Harling was ordered to accompany him. Just as they had entered North King Street, Seán Howard let out a scream. He had been shot by a British sniper and died cradled in Harling's arms. It was left to a very young Seán Harling to go up to Temple buildings to tell Howard's mother. Seán Howard was only fourteen years old.

The following day, Thursday, the local parish priest arrived at the post. He took Paddy Houlihan severely to task for using children in the rebellion and demanded that he order them home. When Houlihan ignored his request, the priest turned to Harling and Tweedale and said, 'You're too young for this, boys. Go on home.' And to make sure they went home, he escorted them as far as Constitution Hill, telling them in a clear commanding voice, 'Be on your way now, boys, and don't come back.'

But Harling sneaked back the next day and was there for the surrender on the Saturday. Harling described the British captain who accepted their surrender as a decent sort of chap, who walked along the line of volunteers, kicking their surrendered guns aside while looking each one in the eye. He sighed when he came to Harling at the end of the line and shook his head, then gave him a clip across the ear and told him to go on off home with himself. Harling was very annoyed at not being arrested, but that was the situation and all he could do was stand and watch his older comrades being marched away. He came back to the barricade the next day and returned the damaged cab to the builder's yard.

Another member of Fianna Éireann killed in action that Easter week was young Seán Healy, who was fifteen years old and lived near Doyle's corner in Phibsborough, just up the road from where Harling lived.

In the aftermath of the insurrection and the execution of Seán Heuston, for whom Harling and his comrades sorely grieved, the Dublin Brigade of the Fianna was disbanded. Heuston, who worked in the Kingsbridge railway station, commanded the men in the Mendicity Institute, who, it is said, fought extremely well. Harling said of him, 'He was our leader, a great man, and an ordinary army would never have executed a young man like Seán Heuston.'

More than six months passed without a murmur of the Dublin Fianna being resurrected. The boys of the North Dublin District became despondent, convinced that the British had effectively crushed the Dublin Brigade. But in December 1916, Harling was told by a friend, Tommy Maken, that a company of Fianna was being reorganised by Peadar Brown and would be parading at 28 North Frederick Street. He immediately joined Brown's company.

When the Dublin Brigade was eventually resurrected in 1917, Harling was transferred to A Company, North City District, whose OC was Liam Murphy. A Company paraded at Skipper's Alley. Periodically the police or the military raided the hall. Members were arrested and held in various jails throughout the country for weeks and months. Harling, however, always managed to escape.

During 1917, the British army carried on a massive recruiting campaign and the whole city was covered with posters showing Lord Kitchener with his finger pointing and a caption that read, 'Britons – We Want You'. The Fianna boys were ordered to destroy or deface as many of them as they could. Harling's commandant came to him one day and said, 'I have been instructed to get you to destroy the recruiting poster that is hanging across the GPO.' Harling went down to have a look at it and, when he saw the gigantic poster draped across the whole length of the building at the very top, nearly collapsed. He thought, 'How the hell am I going to destroy that thing?'

But he got an idea. He went into a shop, bought a sod of turf and left it steeping in a bucket of paraffin oil. With the assistance of a couple of his companions, he wrapped a length of wire around the sod, then tied some twine to the wire, set fire to the turf and flung it up across the banner. It was in flames almost immediately and the fire brigade quickly arrived. When the fireman in charge, Joe Connolly, whose brother Seán was killed in the 1916 rising, saw what was burning he instructed his men to return to base.

One afternoon some time in 1918, Michael Collins had just finished doing some business in the Fianna Éireann headquarters in North Great George's Street when Harling overheard him saying to two IRA officers that they would go over to Vaughan's hotel in Parnell Square. About ten minutes later an excited and out-of-breath Fianna boy came crashing through the door, shouting, 'The British soldiers have Parnell Square cordoned off and are making house-to-house searches there!'

Harling recalled, 'I hopped on my bike and cycled around to survey the situation, but my heart sank when I saw there was really no escape for Collins and his men. I then went on around to Parnell Street but there was no escape route. I cycled on up Dominic Street but could see no way out there either. Disheartened, I decided to go into the church to say a prayer for them. I parked my bike at the railings and on my way in I noticed a little gate at the Dominic Street side of the church. I went over to have a look and to my surprise the gate led to the laneway where Matt Talbot had died. To my further surprise it also seemed to lead to the back of Vaughan's hotel.

'Realising the possibility of an escape route I excitedly tried the gate but it was locked. I then ran into the church and located the parish priest in the vestry. I hurriedly explained the situation to him. He agreed to help and opened the gate for me, then gave me the keys and told me to lock the gate when my business was finished and leave the keys back in the vestry. I sneaked down the lane into which the back yards of the big houses on Dominic Street and Parnell Square crept and there wasn't a sign of a British soldier about. I clambered over the wall at the back of Vaughan's and a porter led me to the room Collins and his staff were meeting in. "Come on, Mick," I shouted. "I've found a way out."

'Collins and his crew didn't hesitate. They followed me out straight away. I locked the gate and left the keys back in the vestry and we left the church through the Dorset Street gate. Collins told us to split up and meet him in a pub in Bachelor's Walk. When we met in the pub Collins jokingly said to me, "You sneaky little whore you, Harling." Then he patted me on the head and said, "Well done. If you were old enough to drink, I'd buy you a pint."'

During the 1918 election Harling went back to the coach-builder's yard near the North Dublin Union with four of his companions and took out the old coach they had used in the barricade during the rising. They borrowed a horse and canvassed around the town, shouting, 'Come and vote in the 1916 cab!' They were canvassing for Michael Staines, who was running against John Dillon Nugent, a Redmondite.

One night they went to Nugent's house, a red-bricked building at the corner of Rathdown Road, Cabra, and daubed the walls with white lead paint. It read, 'Vote for Staines on the wall.' Just as they had finished, Nugent stuck his head out of a window, only to get a paintbrush stuck in his mouth by Volunteer Paddy O'Hanrahan.

Nugent must have had a phone, because when the gang were running up the Phibsborough Road they were confronted by a squad of police blocking their way. They threw what was left of the paint over the police, escaped through a short cut and found refuge in a safe house for the night.

Young Seán Harling, because of his loyalty and diligence to duty, made a positive impression on the leaders of the republican movement and was selected to take charge of twenty young men to police the Mansion House for the first Dáil Éireann sitting and subsequent sittings. Michael Collins was so impressed by the way the policing of the Mansion House was organised that he went to Diarmuid O'Hegarty, secretary of the Dáil, and asked who was in charge of it. After that Harling was given positions of responsibility and trust.

In the first quarter of 1919 he was promoted to lieutenant and transferred to C Company, North City Fianna, in North Summer Street, whose OC was Seán Caffrey. In December 1919, he took part in a raid of destruction on the office of the *Independent* newspaper on Middle Abbey Street. The raid was a sequel to the failed ambush on Lord French on the Ashtown Road by Martin Savage, who was killed:

> Martin Savage unafraid, with rifle and grenade,
> Attacked them without aid on Ashtown Road.
> But a bullet laid him low, from a rifle of the foe.
> That's another death we owe for Ashtown Road.

Harling said that 'although it was widely understood that the Fianna was the youth organisation of the Irish Volunteers and later of the IRA, the Fianna was an independent republican organisation with its own constitution and code of conduct and carried out its own military activities independently of the IRA and others. But their role in the struggle for Irish freedom, like that of Cumann na mBan, was never properly recognised by historians.' Harling was promoted to commandant of the Second Battalion, Dublin Brigade in December 1919 and selected as a member for the Fianna Circle of the IRB.

That same December Garry Houlihan, OC of the Dublin Brigade, and centre of the Fianna Circle, was instructed by Michael Collins to order Seán Harling to report to Diarmuid O'Hegarty at 76 Harcourt Street, where Dáil Éireann was operating underground, to take up a position as courier in his office – a full-time job at a weekly wage of two pounds. O'Hegarty was secretary of Dáil Éireann and director of organisation staff.

In January 1920, the office was raided by the British military and Diarmuid O'Hegarty was arrested. Following this raid they moved to the north side of the River Liffey, to 22 Mary Street, above the shop of Messrs Hogg and Robinson, seed merchants. Michael Collins, as minister for finance, had his office in this building too.

Diarmuid O'Hegarty, who had been sentenced to six months' imprisonment, was released after serving four months, reported to the new office and resumed his position as secretary of Dáil Éireann.

They moved from the Mary Street office after two months to a bigger room over the premises of the Leyland Rubber Company in Middle Abbey Street. The office staff comprised O'Hegarty,

Éamon Price, Molly Ryan, a Miss Hogan and Seán Harling. The Department of Finance remained in Mary Street.

The other Dáil departments were located in streets of close proximity: the Department of Agriculture was in Earl Street, the Ministry of Home Affairs in Henry Street and the Department of Local Government in Clare Street. Cathal Brugha performed his ministerial duties from his business office in Messrs Lalor, candle manufacturers, on Ormond Quay. The office of the adjutant general, Gearóid O'Sullivan, was four doors away from Brugha's.

It was Harling's duty to carry all dispatches for mobilising Dáil Éireann to the above offices and to arrange the printing for the headed paper of the different Dáil departments. At the same time, however, he was working for Collins' HQ staff organising dispatches for his various company units.

'This was very dangerous work,' he said, 'as I was carrying official dispatches, for an outlawed government and for a private army, from early morning 'til late at night. And any risks run by the HQ staff and members of the Dáil were equally shared by me.'

Harling was responsible for notifying the country TDs by letter whenever the Dáil was to be assembled. As the British post could not be trusted, he would write to the girls assigned to assist the TDs telling each that he would meet her in Dublin at a particular time, as if making a date. Each girl would pass the letter to her TD, who knew he was being called to a Dáil meeting. They always met initially in Forrester's hall in Parnell Square (now the Kevin Barry memorial hall), where Harling would tell them the address of the Dáil session. It was nearly always Alderman Cole's big house on Mountjoy Square.

Shortly after moving to Middle Abbey Street, Harling was

made brigade quartermaster of the Dublin Fianna and took charge of the department's dump at North Brunswick Street, where all-important files, army orders and a quantity of arms and ammunition were kept.

The courier system they operated worked well until, one day, two members of Harling's brigade were taken in for questioning by the British military. This led Michael Collins to suspect that some of them were being followed, so he decided to change the system to a more centralised one.

Collins proposed at a ministry meeting that a tobacconist's shop be purchased and given to Harling to run. From there Collins could control all communications. But Harling, being only eighteen years of age and keenly adventurous, did not like the idea of being cooped up in a shop all day long. The next morning he told Collins that he had an unemployed brother, Frank, who had a small shop premises at 96 Upper Church Street, and that he was certain Frank could be persuaded to take control of communications under his own supervision. Collins thought this was a good idea, but there was a problem. Frank was not a member of any nationalist organisation. Collins told Seán that he should first inform his brother of the grave personal risk and danger he would be under if he took on this job. Seán did so. Frank Harling agreed to take the job and was placed on a salary.

Harling's place of abode, adjacent to the Broadstone railway station (the 'gateway to the west'), had not escaped Collins' attention either. He decided to trust Harling with the supervision of another very secret and vital communications system. On 20 October 1920, Collins ordered Harling to take over and organise on an efficient footing all western communications, which up until then had been looked after by Joe Claffey and Patrick Killian, train drivers. Now, with the allegiance of all urban- and county-council bodies to Dáil Éireann having been declared, and the IRA about to be organised into divisions, it was of great importance that these lines of communication be efficiently established under Dáil control. The Broadstone was an excellent position from which Collins could keep in touch with the western commands.

Collins instructed that all goods and passenger trains in and out of the Broadstone would have to be used for this very important work. Harling was to ensure that all those given the task of conveying dispatches were absolutely trustworthy. He agreed with Collins that his own home address was the safest and most appropriate place for delivering and collecting this correspondence. Having secured his mother's willing agreement to this arrangement, Harling went about the task of recruiting his couriers.

Patrick Killian and Joe Claffey agreed to continue carrying dispatches. Thomas O'Neill, a Mr Morgan and two others, all train drivers, were also recruited and a platform staff of four porters was set up and charged with the task of meeting all incoming goods and passenger trains involved in the operations, collecting the return dispatches and dropping them in to Harling's mother. Harling's mother, in turn, was to bring them down to the communications centre in Church Street for final delivery. Through this method a letter from any of the western commands would reach Church Street within four hours. The communications coming through the Broadstone station were from republican army units, TDs, public bodies and the numerous other organisations working for a free and independent Ireland and subject to the Dáil. Each communication bore its own special mark of designation.

This was a smoothly run operation. For example, within a few hours Michael Collins had received the news of the wounding and capture of Seán McKeon by the Auxiliaries at Mullingar railway station. A report about the rescue of Brigadier Frank Carty from Sligo prison, an operation Collins was most anxious about, was sent on the midnight goods train by Brigadier Billy Pilkington of Sligo town and collected by Seán Harling at 4 a.m. at Liffey Junction.

The communications centre at 96 Upper Church Street, supervised and controlled by Seán Harling and run by his brother Frank, assisted by his mother and also by his sister Marcella, worked perfectly for Dáil Éireann and other republican organisations throughout the whole of the war of independence. Dublin Castle never suspected it as having any connection with the cause of Irish freedom.

Before I end this chapter I must relate a humorous story that happened, according to Harling, during the war of independence. Two young volunteers from the Oola district, County Tipperary, came up with a novel idea to raise funds for their unit. They brought a statue of Jesus Christ to a watchmaker pal of theirs and got him to fix the working parts of an alarm clock inside it. They then took the rubber filler from an old fountain pen, filled it with sheep's blood and placed it inside the statue. When the clock struck a certain time it would send out a spurt of blood through our lord's heart. They brought the statue to an old woman's barn in Oola and told her to go to the village and raise the alarm every time the statue bled. When the people came to view it the two IRA lads charged an entrance fee. When the county's bishop was told about the miracle, however, he put a quick stop to their scam.

Chapter 3

De Valera's Man:
According to Seán Harling

One evening, about a week before Christmas 1920, Harling received a note from Michael Collins bearing instructions to meet him at 22 Mary Street at ten o'clock sharp the next morning. Aware of Collins' attitude to tardy volunteers, he left nothing to chance and arrived early. Collins told Harling that his job at Dáil Éireann was finished. 'Dev' had returned from his tour of the United States and had set up his secret headquarters at the house of a Dr Farnham, 5 Merrion Square. Harling had been assigned to Dev's personal staff to work as his confidential courier. He was to continue running western communications for Collins at the same time. Collins instructed Harling to report to de Valera that day and made it very clear that while he was working for the president he must never carry a gun.

Éamon de Valera, being on the run, arrived from America in disguise. He had grown a full moustache and was passing himself off as Captain Hayden, a retired British army officer, and had the papers to prove it.

Harling arrived at Dr Farnham's at 3.30 p.m. He was admitted by Mrs Farnham, who said, 'So you are Seán.' She took him to the rear of the house and knocked on a door, which was opened by Kathleen O'Connell, de Valera's private secretary.

Harling had barely entered the room when de Valera came to him and shook his hand warmly, saying, 'I have already been told about you and your family, Seán, and I am pleased to have you on my staff. Now let me explain your duties. You will be involved in very confidential and secret work; your hours of duty will be most uncertain; there will not be any regular routine. You will be involved mostly in outdoor duties, including the convening of the republican cabinet for weekly cabinet meetings.'

When the meeting ended, de Valera walked him to the door and said, 'I'll expect to see you at about 10 a.m. tomorrow, but you will first call on secretary Diarmuid O'Hegarty at Broadway, O'Connell Street, and collect any correspondence for me there.'

Harling, save for Kathleen O'Connell, was the only person in direct contact with de Valera, and he and Miss O'Connell attended to all the president's needs. As he had been ordered by Collins always to be available to de Valera, it was necessary for Harling to reside at Dr Farnham's house.

After only about a week working for the president, Harling was travelling down Mount Street in a tram when the British army set up a roadblock at the end of the street and began stopping and searching people. Harling jumped off the tram to head back up the street, but to his horror saw that the British had erected another barricade there too. He was in a tight corner because, in defiance of Collins' orders, he was carrying a Webley pistol. He was hurriedly looking for a way out when he spotted a girl standing at a door with a baby in her arms. He took a chance and approached the girl, saying, 'Look, I'm in a jam. I have a gun and I want it hidden for a while.' The girl, without hesitating, said, 'Come on upstairs.'

They entered a room where a middle-aged woman was sitting and the girl said, 'Mother, this is Jim.' The mother returned a cheerful, 'Hello, Jim.' The girl took the gun and hid it. Harling went back for it the next day, but he never again set eyes on the girl.

When travelling by tram with ministerial documents, he always took the front seat at the top. There was a box there that housed the name of where the tram was going and the trap door leading to it was always open. From that position he also had a clear view of the street below. If a military lorry pulled up and the soldiers boarded the tram to search the passengers, Harling would quickly stuff the documents into the little box. It never failed.

Correspondence of lesser importance would be inserted inside a copy of the *London Illustrated News*. If the tram was held up by British forces, Harling would throw the paper on the rack and stand up to be searched. This ploy's rationale was that the British soldiers would be unlikely to suspect anyone reading the *London Illustrated News* of being a republican courier, and it always proved successful too.

They left Dr Farnham's house after a fortnight there and went to one called Loughnavale, on Strand Road in Sandymount. Maura McGarry, de Valera's housekeeper, had bought this house from Dáil Éireann funds in her own name.

One evening in February 1921, Harling was returning from town to Loughnavale with the president's American mail (a bulky lot, which included a very important cinematograph film of de Valera's tour of America and two records of his speeches there), which he had collected from Collins' office. He alighted from the tram and was about to proceed along Sydney Parade when he saw a Crossley Tender full of Black and Tans coming towards him from the Sandymount direction. Luckily, he had made a parcel of his bulky correspondence while on the tram. He threw it over a garden wall at the corner of Ailesbury Road and stood there praying that the Tender would pass him by. It did not.

The vehicle stopped. Two Tans got out and asked him what

he was doing there. He told them he was awaiting a tram for Kingstown. Then, having searched him, they proceeded to rain blows upon him. They punched him to the ground and began kicking him. He was almost unconscious when he heard a voice from the lorry shouting, 'Don't stay there all night!' The two Tans, having threatened to shoot Harling, got back into the Tender and drove away, splitting their sides with laughter.

Blinded by pain, Harling retrieved the mail and arrived back at the president's house, sporting two black eyes, a bloody nose and a puffed face, but with the mail and film safe. De Valera tended to his injuries and expressed in no uncertain terms his disgust at the treatment meted out to him by the Tans. He gave Harling the film of his American tour as a souvenir.

Joseph O'Reilly of Collins' staff, who became a colonel in the Free State army, took over Harling's duties for the few days he was indisposed.

They spent four months at Loughnavale then moved to a house called Glenvar, on Mount Merrion Avenue in Blackrock. Before they occupied it, Batt O'Connor, a building contractor, built a secret dump with a very clever opening and closing mechanism. Each night, before curfew, all documents and correspondence were picked up off the floor and placed in a deed box, which was then put into the dump in the rockery. The deed box was always taken out in the morning and left on the study floor during the day.

From the time de Valera came home from America until the truce in July 1921, he was inundated with requests for interviews from prominent and influential people, such as foreign diplomats and journalists from the likes of the *International News*, *Echo de Paris*, the Hearst press and many British journals and newspapers. It was

Harling's responsibility to arrange safe houses and to convey those who were granted interviews to the meetings. He took precautions to ensure that neither he nor any of these people were followed by British agents and that none of them was a government agent. Before an interview was granted, the applicant was thoroughly checked by Collins' Department of Intelligence. Though Harling received personal directions from Collins about the safety of the president, final arrangements were always made through Harling himself.

He would meet Collins in town every morning to arrange the day's work ahead for de Valera. For example, if Collins told him that the Hearst press in America was seeking an interview, Harling would go back and ask de Valera if he would grant it. If de Valera agreed, Harling would arrange a safe house in which the interview could take place. Most of the foreign journalists stayed in the Shelbourne hotel. Harling would go there, pick them up at an arranged time and convey them to the meeting.

He always used two cars owned by Batty and Joe Hyland. Harling would send one for de Valera and use the other one himself to pick up the journalist. He always made sure that the president arrived first. Batty Hyland, driving de Valera, would wait until he saw Harling's car coming along the street, then move off.

One morning, Collins sent Harling to meet Fr Michael O'Flanagan at the home of Councillor Paul in Common Street. Fr O'Flanagan told him that Sir James Craig, the first prime minister of Northern Ireland, was in town as a guest of Lord Justice O'Connor, and wished to meet with the president. De Valera agreed and sent Harling to Lord Justice O'Connor's home to arrange the meeting. Satisfied that all was in order, he instructed Sir James to be ready at ten o'clock the next morning.

Sir James was ready and waiting when Harling arrived and

he took him to the house of a sympathetic solicitor near Sutton Cross. When passing through Clontarf, Sir James asked, 'Would it be indiscreet if I asked where I am?'

'No sir, you are in Clontarf.'

'Oh,' Craig remarked, 'this is where King Brian fought the Danes.'

The interview lasted half an hour and Harling brought Sir James back to Lord Justice O'Connor's house. Later that evening, the driver of the Belfast mail train handed Harling a poster published by the *Belfast News Letter*, bearing in large letters the words, 'Sir James Now in the Camp of the Enemy'.

When Lord Derby came to town he took up residence in the Gresham hotel under the name of Mr Edwards. Through the offices of Mr Cope, the under secretary for Ireland, he sought an interview with de Valera. Michael Collins contacted Harling and instructed him to inform de Valera that Lord Derby wanted to meet him. De Valera granted the interview and sent Harling along to make arrangements.

When Harling entered the hotel he sought out Charlie Price, the head waiter there and a member of Michael Collins' intelligence staff, whose sister was married to Tom Barry. Price gave him the number of Lord Derby's suite. Harling knocked on the door, which was opened by an English protestant minister who had accompanied Lord Derby over from England.

Harling announced, boldly and mischievously, 'I was sent by the president of the Irish republic to see Mr Edwards.'

'You cannot see Mr Edwards,' was the reply. 'Any business you have with him will have to be conveyed through me.'

'If I cannot see Lord Derby then the matter would have to end here, for my instructions are to deal with Lord Derby personally.'

The minister, clearly annoyed, called him an impudent pup and said, 'Do you realise that the fate of a nation is in your hands?'

'Your remarks do not impress me. My instructions are to see Mr Edwards only.'

Just then a tall, heavily built man emerged from the inner room and invited him in. The man was Lord Derby. Harling informed him that the interview had been granted and that he would return at 7 p.m. to take him to the president.

When he left the hotel he hurried over to Diarmuid O'Hegarty's office to select the nearest safe house. He deemed the big house belonging to O'Mara, the bacon curer from Limerick, in Fitzwilliam Square to be the safest. He went there and arranged for the use of the house for that night with the housekeeper. Then he went to the home of Batty and Joe Hyland in Denzille Lane to book their cars for the evening.

Harling returned to Glenvar to inform de Valera that all the arrangements were in place, and he dutifully told him about the protestant minister. De Valera told him that under no circumstances was the minister to be brought to the interview.

When Harling called for Lord Derby that evening, the minister was ready to accompany him. Harling told him that the interview was only between Lord Derby and the president, but the minister insisted on tagging along. Harling was in two minds about whether to abort the meeting when he spotted Charlie Price in the vestibule. He went over to Charlie and told him to come and tell the minister he was wanted in the reception room. Charlie cheerfully did as he was bidden. When the minister went to the reception room, Harling ushered Lord Derby out the door, into Joe Hyland's car and away. As they were pulling away, Lord Derby remarked, 'That was a neat little trick you pulled back there.'

The interview lasted an hour and his lordship was most profuse in his thanks when Harling dropped him off at the Gresham.

When General Smuts came to town he stayed in the Shelbourne and met de Valera at Dr Farnham's house. He later remarked that he got a bit of a shock when Harling came to arrange the meeting with de Valera, for he couldn't believe that a man of his stature and one who looked so young could hold such an important position in the republican movement. De Valera also met with Archbishop Clune in early December 1920.

Some time in the middle of June 1921, de Valera wished to visit Maynooth College on special business with the bishop of Dublin. Harling arranged for Batty Hyland to pick them up at Glenvar. Before they drove off, de Valera asked Batty if he knew the way through Stillorgan and Terenure to the Clondalkin Road. He wished, for security reasons, to travel that way. Batty said he did. But when they reached the Clondalkin Road, Batty took a wrong turn, bringing them uncomfortably close to the gate of Baldonnel aerodrome, which was occupied by the Black and Tans.

Harling and de Valera were seated in the back, de Valera just behind the driver. A Tan officer carrying a machine-gun approached the car on Harling's side and questioned them as to why they were at the barracks. De Valera reached over Harling, showing his identification as Captain Hayden, and explained to the officer that they were on their way to Lucan and had taken a wrong turn.

The officer eyed them suspiciously, machine-gun at the ready, then stood back on the path and instructed Batty to turn the car around very slowly and pull up beside him. Batty drove towards the gate of the barracks and turned the car ever so slowly, watching the inside of the gate while Harling peered along both sides of the fence. There was no sign of any other Tan either immediately inside the gate or anywhere along the perimeter.

Batty pulled up beside the Tan officer, who began questioning de Valera, then glanced back at Harling with an expression that said, 'What are we going to do here, Seán?' They were under strict orders from Collins that under no circumstances, no matter what they had to do, should they allow de Valera to be captured. Harling very slowly and carefully took his Webley pistol from his pocket – the one that the girl in Mount Street had hidden for him, and the one he had been instructed by Collins never to carry – and slipped it to Batty unbeknown to de Valera.

The Tan officer was only inches away from Batty, his head bent down. If he made a move to arrest de Valera, Batty would be able to shoot him and escape before help could arrive. But to their relief, the Tan officer turned to Batty and gave him directions for the Lucan Road. While de Valera was thanking him, Hyland slipped the gun back to Harling. They had had a narrow escape, and de Valera had no idea what the two were up to. They never told him, nor did they ever tell Collins.

They pulled up on the Kilcock Road when they reached Maynooth. Harling got out, crossed the road and climbed over the wall into the grounds. There he met the Reverend Dr Brown and told him that the president was outside and wished to know the quietest way to enter. Dr Brown told him the best way would be through the front gates. The president conducted his business with the bishop and they returned to Glenvar without further incident.

On Thursday evening, 22 June 1921, Harling called to see Cathal Brugha at Lalor's candle factory, Ormond Quay, where Brugha gave him a document for the president headed, 'Dáil Éireann,

Dept. of Defence'. Brugha instructed Harling to take the greatest care of the document, which contained many suggestions for intensifying the military campaign.

When Harling left Brugha's office he strolled to Nelson's pillar, hopped on a tram for Blackrock Park and arrived there at 8.30 p.m. He took the precaution of going up Mount Merrion Avenue to enter Glenvar by the Cross Avenue gate. After the customary conversations with the president, he handed over the document from the minister for defence.

Harling was working in the study with the president, and Kathleen O'Connell was entertaining Maura McGarry, when he happened to look out the window and see a detachment of British soldiers stretched across the meadow and advancing towards the house. He alerted the president. De Valera looked out the window, then turned to Harling, who was in the process of picking up the deed box.

'Leave that, Seán!' he cried. 'We've no time to dump it now. You go and make well your escape. I'll bluff these fellows.'

Harling jumped out of a window and ran across the back field to the grounds of Professor MacNeill's house and then out onto Nutley Avenue. His plan was to try and make it to the house of Nicholas Kelly, the then OC of the Blackrock Fianna, before curfew.

He headed towards Carysfort Avenue in the hope that he could find somewhere to hide in Blackrock. Curfew time was a dangerous time for anyone to be abroad, and a volunteer's instructions were clearly defined – he was to reach safety at all costs. Upon reaching the top of Carysfort Avenue he encountered a British foot patrol moving towards the Stillorgan Road. He entered the garden of a house and concealed himself in the shrubbery until the patrol had passed. When they had gone, he made it to Blackrock.

The place was completely deserted, the only sign of life being at the old Dublin United tram depot, and it was there that he decided to seek shelter for the night. But he was confronted by the nightwatchman (who, he later learned, was a Mr Lee, a friend of Nicholas Kelly's), who thought he was a thief and threatened to alert the soldiers. Harling frantically explained that he was from the city and had left a girl home to Blackrock, but had delayed too long and was caught out by the curfew. The watchman seemed to doubt him at first, but told him he could bunk down in any of the trams at the back.

Harling found it hard to sleep that night. When curfew lifted at 5 a.m., he ran all the way back to Glenvar and roused the gardener, who lived in the Cross Avenue lodge. The gardener told him the raiders were gone.

He entered the house and was confronted by Maura McGarry, who was crying and anxiously awaiting his return. She informed him that 'the chief' and Kathleen O'Connell had been arrested and explained what had happened.

De Valera, as Captain Hayden, had engaged the officer in charge of the raiding party in conversation in the study while his men had searched the house. They had found nothing, but when the sergeant had entered the study to report to his officer he had tripped over the deed box on the floor. Some papers had fallen out, and the very first one they picked up was the message from Cathal Brugha stating how he was about to intensify the campaign.

'These documents appear to be of a very seditious nature, Mr Hayden,' the officer had informed de Valera. 'I will have to take you to Dublin Castle.' Kathleen O'Connell had stepped forward and told the officer that the deed box and its contents were hers.

'No,' de Valera had interrupted, 'they are mine.'

'We won't argue about them,' said the officer. 'Both of you had better come along.'

It was now 6 a.m. Harling told Maura McGarry to wait in the house in case anyone came with information while he cycled over to Donnybrook to find Michael Collins and report the incident to him.

He called on Batt O'Connor to tell him what had happened and to find out where Michael Collins was. O'Connor brought him to 6 Brendan Road, which they entered through the back door. Collins told Harling that he had already been notified about the arrests by his agents in Dublin Castle and that the president had been sent from the castle to Portobello barracks.

They had breakfast in O'Connor's, then Collins gave Harling the address of a safe house on the Rathmines Road. He was to go and stay there until a certain person came to the house from the barracks with information.

Harling knocked on the door of the house, which was directly facing Military Road, and when challenged said, 'I was sent by Michael Collins.' He was ushered into the front sitting-room without any questions being asked.

It was 10 a.m. when he sat down at the window, where he had a clear view of Military Road. A few minutes later he saw a civilian workman emerge through the gates of the barracks and cross the road towards the house. He heard the man knock five times on the door before it was opened. Seconds later the man was standing at the door of the room where Harling sat.

'Were you sent here by Mick Collins?' asked the man.

'Yes, I was,' answered Harling.

'Well, you can tell the Big Fellow that the Long Fellow is having a posh time of it in officers' quarters. But if you hang on I might have some news for you later in the morning.' The man returned to the barracks just as quickly as he had come, leaving Harling wondering what he meant. How could de Valera be having a 'posh time of it'? He decided not to bother Collins with that information but to wait for developments of a more concrete nature.

At about twelve noon the same man returned and told Harling that the 'Long Fellow' was being released and would be coming out shortly. No sooner had the man left when Harling observed Éamon de Valera and a staff officer walk down Military Road, stop at the corner, have a short chat, shake hands, then part company. As he watched de Valera walk towards Portobello bridge, Harling thought, 'What the hell was all that about?'

He left the house, intending to make contact with de Valera at some point along the road, but the president jumped onto a passing tram bound for Dartry and Harling missed him. He gave a full account of what had happened to Michael Collins, who instructed him not to go to Glenvar until he himself had had contact with the president.

That evening Harling received a note from de Valera telling him not to go anywhere near Glenvar, as he did not want Harling to become known to the British as his assistant. That evening Harling met Collins, who told him that he was to retire to the background and that another job was being arranged for him. Harling later learned that de Valera had been arrested in error – the British had had a peace offer in the offing.

On the morning of Saturday, 24 June, Harling reported to the general secretary's office in O'Connell Street, where Diarmuid O'Hegarty told him that he was to take over the secret Dáil registry at 117 North King Street, starting the following Monday. He then went to the Broadstone station in connection with western communications. After that, at about 11.30 a.m., he called to the clearing house in Church Street, where his brother Frank informed him that the lord mayor of Dublin, Alderman Laurence O'Neill, had earlier sent his valet Buckley to Harling's home in Phibsborough with the message that the lord mayor wanted to see him urgently.

Harling arrived at the Mansion House some time after noon. The lord mayor greeted him and informed him that a British staff officer from Dublin Castle was waiting there with an important confidential letter from David Lloyd George, British prime minister. The lord mayor was reluctant to take responsibility for the letter, addressed to 'Éamon de Valera, Representative of the Irish People, Mansion House, Dublin, Ireland', unless he could be assured of its safe delivery to the president. Harling gave him that assurance.

The lord mayor handed Harling a large buff envelope containing the letter. He examined it carefully. On the lower corner was printed, 'If undelivered return to 10 Downing Street, London.' 'O.H.M.S.' was written on the top.

Harling, remembering that Saturday was a half day at the secretariat, rushed down to Nassau Street and arrived there after 1 p.m., but the office was already closed. This posed a dilemma for him: although he had the letter he also had instructions not to go near Glenvar. However, he considered the letter to be of the utmost importance in the struggle for Irish freedom, so he decided to take a chance, go out to Glenvar and contact the president personally.

Taking the proper precautions, he boarded the Kingstown tram and alighted at Blackrock Park. While he was making his way up Mount Merrion Avenue, intending to enter the house by the

Cross Avenue gate, he met de Valera hurrying down from Glenvar towards him, minus his moustache. He had just shaved it off.

De Valera told him that he was hurrying to Blackrock railway station to catch the 2.30 p.m. train to Greystones, where he intended to spend the weekend with his family. Harling told de Valera what had happened and handed him the envelope. De Valera opened the letter and read it. After a few moments he said, 'This letter certainly alters my plans for the weekend.' Then he remarked, 'It looks, Seán, as if we will be in the viceregal lodge soon, but at the moment we have a heavy evening before us.'

They returned to Glenvar and upon entering the study de Valera asked, 'What are the chances of a cabinet meeting for tonight, Seán?' Harling didn't know, but assured him that he could contact O'Hegarty and some of the ministers.

'Do the best you can, Seán,' de Valera told him. 'I will be available for any arrangements made.'

The calling of a cabinet meeting with a week's notice was a headache enough for Harling, but the calling of one with only a moment's notice could prove well-nigh impossible. No written communications were issued when a cabinet meeting was called, which meant that he had to contact each minister personally. He knew that W. T. Cosgrave lived in Templeogue and Count Plunkett in Bray, for example, but since they were all on the run the task of finding out where any of them were staying would be a trying one. Only Michael Collins ever left word where he was going. However, it had to be done.

Harling went into Dublin, arriving there about 3.30 p.m., and went directly to Archer's of Shannon Road. There he met Diarmuid O'Hegarty and told him of the letter and of what the president required. O'Hegarty said he was meeting Collins at Vaughan's hotel at 6 p.m. and that Harling was to contact whatever ministers he could in the meantime and return to let him know. Harling was successful in contacting Austin Stack, Cathal Brugha and W. T. Cosgrave.

Cabinet meetings were usually held at 40 Herbert Park or 36 Ailesbury Road and it was usual for the president to go to these meetings on a push-bike with Harling pedalling alongside him.

This meeting was held at Herbert Park, and the ministers quickly decided that the text of the Downing Street letter should appear in all the Sunday papers. The curfew was on but they had, somehow, to get the text into the press the next morning. Harling phoned the different papers and asked their representatives to come and meet him at a carefully selected safe house, one on the corner of Mount Merrion Avenue, owned by a Miss Macken.

It was from there that the text of the letter was given to each Dublin newspaper with instructions that it must appear in the Sunday-morning issues. Each paper went to considerable trouble to comply with the cabinet's wishes. Next morning the publications duly appeared.

The text of the letter read:

Sir
The British Government are deeply anxious that, so far as they can assure it, the King's appeal for reconciliation in Ireland shall not have been made in vain. Rather than allow another opportunity of settlement in Ireland to be cast aside, they feel it incumbent upon them to make a final appeal in the spirit of the King's words for a conference between themselves and the representatives of Southern and Northern Ireland.

I write, therefore, to convey the following invitation to you as the chosen leader of the great majority in Southern Ireland and to Sir James Craig, the Premier of Northern Ireland. (1) That you should attend a conference here in London in the company of

Sir James Craig, to explore to the utmost the possibility of a settlement: (2) That you should bring with you for the purpose any colleague whom you may select. The Government will, of course, give a safe conduct to all who may be chosen to participate in the conference.

We make this invitation with a fervent desire to end the ruinous conflict which for centuries divided Ireland and embittered the relations of the peoples of these two islands, who ought to live in neighbourly harmony with each other, and whose co-operation would mean so much not only to the empire but to humanity:

We wish that no endeavour should be lacking on our part to realise the King's prayer, and we ask you to meet us, as we will meet you, in the spirit of conciliation for which his Majesty appealed.

I am sir, your obedient servant,

D. Lloyd George

The next day, 26 June 1921, expecting hostilities to break out again if the outcome of the negotiations was not successful, de Valera ordered Harling to go underground so as not to become known to Dublin Castle as de Valera's aide, but promised that he would keep in secret contact with him from then on, no matter what form future events might take.

Harling reported back to Diarmuid O'Hegarty, who put him in charge of the files registry of the first Dáil Éireann in North King Street. He continued to control and supervise the dispatches to and from his brother Frank's shop at 96 Upper Church Street.

Although Harling was not visibly working for de Valera any more, he did attend cabinet meetings during the peace negotiations. He recalled being at the cabinet meeting when Collins was selected to go to London to negotiate the Treaty. According to Harling, Collins did not want to go – he saw himself as a soldier and not the type to negotiate a deal. But it was a cabinet decision and he had to, so he demanded that they invest him with full power to reach an agreement.

He also reported that at another meeting after Collins' return with a controversial Treaty agreement, Arthur Griffith said, 'With the Treaty we are able to march into the British empire with our heads up,' and that, in reply, one of the anti-Treaty republicans shouted, 'Mind you don't trip over the fucking mat!'

Just before the vote on the Treaty, on 7 January 1922, Liam Mellows came to Harling and handed him a flag. He told him to go over to O'Connell Street as soon as the vote was taken and, if the result was in favour of the Treaty, hoist this flag over the GPO. It was just after dark. It was a republican flag with a little Union Jack stitched into the corner. I do not recall whether or not Harling told me if he managed to hoist the flag.

Chapter 4

The Redicans

James Redican was born in Keash, County Sligo, in 1891. His parents, Thomas and Anne (Annie), decided to move to Dublin around 1899 or 1900. James and his mother came by train while his father, who was born and reared in a place called the Rock of Doon near Boyle, County Roscommon, cycled all the way.

> Oh, Thomas came by bicycle,
> Annie came by train.
> The wind blew up her petticoat
> And we saw her magazine.

They lived at Nutley Lane in Donnybrook first and it was there that Thomas junior was born in 1901. They later moved to Pembroke cottages, also in Donnybrook. The father, a gardener by trade, worked for people in the Ailesbury Road district and had a fertile vegetable plot in the area. He grew every variety of vegetable known in Ireland at the time and thus saved on the grocery bills, plus made a bit of extra money selling his surplus crop. He was an enthusiastic supporter of James Connolly, although he was not active in any movement. It appears that he was one of the gardeners who planted the trees in O'Connell Street. Dorothy, Patrick and Laurence were born in Pembroke cottages and, like their two older siblings, attended school in Donnybrook.

The father was steeped in Irish traditional music and was an accomplished concert flute player. Laurence and Patrick were the only ones to follow in his footsteps, Laurence taking up the fiddle and banjo and Patrick playing the button accordion, tin whistle and mouth organ. Patrick was also a very good *sean-nós* dancer and, as a young boy, was a drummer in the Irish Citizen Army pipe band, which was later to become the Fintan Lawlor pipe band.

James Redican became a bookmaker's clerk after leaving school and within a few years had graduated to becoming a bookie himself. He opened his shop, 'Bolshiviki' Bookies, under the pseudonym Thomas Casey at 5 Fitzwilliam Terrace, Bray, County Wicklow, where he became known as a colourful and controversial character and also as a ladies' man. He became a volunteer in E Company, Third Battalion, Dublin Brigade, Irish Volunteers and was very badly wounded in the 1916 Easter rising, fighting in Boland's mill near Ringsend alongside his commander, Éamon de Valera. He was captured by the British military and interned in Frongoch prison in Wales.

> One of our leaders was down in Ringsend,
> For the honour of Ireland to uphold and defend.
> He had no veteran soldiers but volunteers raw,
> Playing sweet Mauser music for Erin Go Bragh.
>
> *The Row in the Town*

When James Redican was finally released from Frongoch he did not immediately join the newly formed Irish Republican Army because he was seriously incapacitated (and would be for the rest of his life) by the wounds he had received in Boland's mill. His right arm, hand and ankle were badly damaged, as was his left leg. Though unattached, he did attend parades of the Dublin Brigade, de Valera's own company, when they were held at Donnybrook.

Then, in August 1920, unable to find employment and itching for action, James Redican left Dublin and went to Mullingar, where he joined the South Westmeath Brigade of the IRA, principally because he had friends there, and he was a west of Ireland man himself. He was made commandant-in-charge with the special assignment of raiding banks for the procurement of funds for the brigade's coffers and levying certain rates on farmers throughout the country for Dáil Éireann.

Commandant Redican selected a team of seven men to carry out the bank raids. They were James Gaffney, Christopher Fitzsimons, James Murray, Michael Murray, William Murray, Vice-Commandant Tormey and Thomas Weymes. They carried out their first raid successfully, and with military precision, in the town of Mullingar. And although their sphere of operations did not officially include Dublin, Brigadier T. J. Burke of Mullingar ordered them to move to the big smoke, where they could carry out more lucrative raids.

James Redican, as commandant, was charged with the responsibility of covering the retreat of his men and handing over the money taken to the brigadier. He was armed at all times and was always last to leave the scene of the raid.

When the men from the Westmeath Brigade came to Dublin to carry out bank raids they would hole up in a small hotel in Tara Street owned by a Miss Sullivan, a republican. From there they would set out to raid the selected bank, and there they would return with the loot. Four of them would stand watch on the street corners around the hotel for half an hour after the raid, making sure the military were not on their tail, while Thomas Weymes and James Murray would transfer the loot to an attaché case held by Vice-Commandant Tormey, which he then locked and handed over to Commandant Redican for transfer to Brigadier Burke in Mullingar. Neither Redican nor any of his crew ever counted the money.

On the afternoon of 7 February 1921, the National Bank on Upper Baggot Street was raided by a group of armed men for the second time in just under three months. (The South Westmeath Brigade had raided it on 16 November 1920.) The following evening, Commandant James Redican, masquerading under his bookie's name, Thomas Casey, was arrested at his address in Bray by Inspectors Forrest and Davison and brought to the local police barracks. There he and five other men were paraded in front of two witnesses, one an official at the bank that had been raided, the other a customer who had been on the premises during the raid. They picked out one man as having been one of the raiders, but it was not James Redican.

Instead of releasing Redican, however, the police took him by military escort to the Bridewell police station in Dublin, where he was charged with robbery with force and violence at the National Bank, Upper Baggot Street. He was further charged with shooting at one Alexander McCreary with intent to murder while robbing the same bank, and for shooting at the Auxiliaries with the same intent when they tried to block his escape. He was remanded in custody.

Tom Redican, a robust young boy, earned himself the reputation of being as hard as nails while growing up in the Donnybrook area, because he never backed down in a fight. He loved a good 'scrap', as he described it, and was involved in many of them during his school years. He grew up to become an absolutely fearless man who seemed to be possessed of an almost supernatural self-confidence and whose motto throughout life was, 'A backward step take from no man.'

He had been employed casually as a messenger by traders in the Donnybrook district from when he was about thirteen years of age up until Easter week 1916. When the rising began, Tom Redican, at the tender age of fifteen years, answered the call to arms for Irish freedom. He followed his older brother James into Boland's mill and was looking forward to a good 'scrap' with the British army. But de Valera spoiled it for him on that Tuesday evening. He gave Tom a letter to deliver to Mrs de Valera and ordered him not to come back – he was too young.

According to police records, Tom Redican left Dublin after Easter week and went to Boyle, County Roscommon, where he caused the 'Auxies' there considerable trouble for a few years. Then, in mid-1920, he returned to Dublin with Thomas Weymes and William Murray where he became involved in sporadic skirmishes with the Auxies and the Black and Tans. He took two hits from the Tans during one of these encounters, one in the hand and one in the knee.

While Tom was away causing trouble in Roscommon, his parents and siblings moved to a house at 34 Oxford Road in Ranelagh.

On 1 December 1920, a bitterly cold night, the Tans battered down the front door of the Redicans' home, dragged them out of their beds and made them stand on the cold cobbled floor in their bare feet and flimsy night attire. They shivered with cold, and more so with fear, while the Tans ransacked their home looking for Tom, who they said had been involved in an ambush on one of their patrols that October, and who they believed had been shot and wounded in the affray.

The mother yelled at the captain, 'Get out of my house! Get out of my country!' The captain, taking great exception to this, stood on her bare foot with his hobnailed boot and gave her a crack across the jaw with the butt of his revolver. The boys, lest they be shot dead, did not dare lift a finger to help her.

On 9 December, Thomas was arrested along with a comrade, Paddy Gallagher, a porter at the Broadstone station (but not one of Harling's men), when the lodging house they were billeted in at 4 St Teresa's Terrace, Glasnevin, was raided by the Tans. They were taken first to Collinstown and held there until 23 December, when they were transferred to Arbour Hill and imprisoned without trial for the next couple of months.

They were released on 13 February 1921. Six days later, however, Thomas Redican was arrested at his parents' home in Ranelagh by a Sergeant Killeen. He was three months away from his twentieth birthday. Thomas Weymes of Mullingar was also arrested, and – despite the fact that Tom Redican had been in custody on that date – both were charged with the raid on the National Bank on 7 February. They denied the charge.

Two witnesses, the manager of the bank and the same lady customer as before, were brought to the Bridewell to pick out the raiders from a line-up of ten men. They identified Thomas Weymes first. When the witnesses came to the two Redicans they could not tell them apart.

The woman, pressurised into making a hurried identification, confusedly said that Thomas looked like the man with the gun and that James looked like the man behind the counter. The manager disagreed, saying that Thomas was the man behind the counter and James was the man with the gun. But when asked by the police inspector if he could be more explicit, he replied, 'Well, if he [Thomas] wasn't the man behind the counter, then he must have been the man with the gun.' He appeared to be even more confused than the lady customer. However, the police just wanted confirmation that the brothers had been in the bank during the raid. They were charged and held in custody in Arbour Hill until 11 April, when they were committed for trial by court martial.

To ensure that there would be no contradictory evidence or confusion on the part of the witnesses, two separate trials were held on the same day, 12 May. James Redican was tried by British field general court martial at Kilmainham courthouse. Thomas Redican and Thomas Weymes were tried together by British field general court martial in Richmond barracks, Inchicore, just up the road from Kilmainham.

At James Redican's trial one witness said, 'There was a shot let off in the bank. The men ran out and I heard another shot from outside.' But the witness could not positively identify James Redican as being the gunman.

At the trial of Thomas Redican, a witness said that at 2.15 p.m. on 7 February a man he did not know pointed a pistol at him and ordered him to put his hands up. But that man was not the accused. Another witness who was in the bank on the day of the raid said that he had attended two identity parades but could not identify the accused as being one of the raiders.

However, despite some witnesses not being able to identify them and the confusion of others, the British authorities, it seemed, wanted all three men in custody. James Redican was quickly found guilty and sentenced to penal servitude for life and to suffer eighteen strokes of the cat-o'-nine-tails. The life sentence was later commuted to fifteen years' penal servitude. The flogging was not confirmed. He was thirty-one years of age when convicted and lost his first love because of it.

Thomas Redican and Thomas Weymes were also found guilty and sentenced to twelve years' penal servitude and to suffer twelve strokes of the cat-o'-nine-tails. The flogging was not confirmed. When sentenced, Thomas Redican shouted at the judge, 'How can you convict me of this crime when it was committed on a day when I was still interned in Arbour Hill prison?' He was speedily ushered out of court by half a dozen burly military policemen.

It was revealed at James Redican's court martial that a total of five thousand pounds had been seized in the raids, which was a lot of money at the time. That was the first time, too, that the raiders knew how much they had stolen. But when the IRA checked to see how much of the money had found its way to them, they drew a blank. Considering the fact that they had received nothing from the raids and that James Redican had employed a barrister to defend him, they came to the conclusion that Redican had pocketed the proceeds from the robberies, which were therefore of a criminal nature, and disowned the raiders.

The three men were delivered to Mountjoy jail to commence their sentences in May 1921. They were treated as interned prisoners, being housed with other republican prisoners of war and allowed to wear their own clothes.

Two months after their imprisonment, on 11 July, the truce between Sinn Féin and the British government was signed. On 6 December that year, the plenipotentiaries Collins, Griffith and the rest of the delegation, with the exception of Erskine Childers, signed the Anglo-Irish Treaty. The Treaty was approved by a Dáil majority on 7 January 1922 and the provisional government formally ratified it three days later in the Mansion House.

An amnesty for all political prisoners was granted and, in February 1922, the Redican brothers and Thomas Weymes were released unconditionally along with 150 of their colleagues who had been tried and sentenced by British court martial. The three declared themselves anti-Treaty.

They were destined to enjoy only a couple of weeks' freedom, for certain officers in the Dublin Brigade of the IRA were still smarting over not receiving the money from the bank raids. These were officers whom James Redican had antagonised by ridiculing them for not taking part in the 1916 rising. Indeed, he claimed, some volunteers in the Dublin Brigade who had not turned out in 1916 were jealous, envious and resentful towards him and a few other volunteers who had. It was those officers, according to James Redican, who sent out a group of armed IRA volunteers on the evening of 16 March 1922 to arrest him, his brother and Thomas Weymes and take them to general headquarters, Beggar's Bush barracks, for questioning.

The brothers and Weymes refused to cooperate and James Redican demanded an investigation into what he considered to be a very serious accusation. The three were bundled off to Mountjoy prison once again, James Redican claiming that they were being reinterned for demanding an investigation into their case.

Chapter 5

Fianna Éireann

After the approval of the Treaty, Harling's brother Frank sided with Collins, but Harling himself remained loyal to de Valera and the republic. He was suspended from his job in the Dáil secretariat on 8 July 1922 by Micheál Ó Loingsigh, acting on the instructions of the Dáil clerk, Colm Ó Murchadha. Ó Murchadha had been shown a police report confirming that Harling had become active with the Irregulars. He had been called up for active service at the beginning of July by Fianna Éireann general headquarters to defend the republic and was promoted to officer commanding the Dublin Brigade by the adjutant general, H. C. Mellows (Liam Mellows' brother). He took charge of the intelligence unit of the brigade as well as organising the active-service units.

They took over buildings in North Great George's Street and burrowed their way through them into a bank on the corner, where they found lots of money lying about.

'Like the big eejit I was,' said Harling, 'I sent off a dispatch rider to the bank manager's home in Drumcondra to come and collect the money.' It was a pity, he later joked, that James Redican had not been with him.

Seán Harling first met Dorothy (Nora) Redican, his future wife, during the civil war. She was acting nurse tending the wounded at the Fianna headquarters. Harling had taken time out from the fighting to check on the wounded boys under his command. He asked Nora, whom he didn't know at the time, if everyone was all right. She replied, 'Yes, all except young Clarke over there,' pointing to a body lying on the floor. 'He was shot by a sniper and died a few minutes ago.'

Harling was visibly moved by the news and Nora Redican briefly took his hand in hers in a consoling gesture. He ordered one of the Fianna boys to go and inform young Clarke's parents about their son's death and to have them make arrangements for his funeral. The boy came back with the sad news that young William Clarke had been an orphan and had lived with his aunt, who was very poorly off, could not afford to give him a funeral and requested that the Fianna give him a decent burial. Again, Harling was visibly moved by this news and once more Nora Redican consoled him, this time putting an arm around his waist and drawing him close to her.

Harling felt he had a responsibility to grant the aunt's request. He commandeered a small van and placed the boy's body in the back, then told Nora to get into the seat beside him. He placed his gun on her lap. She looked at him with great surprise and said jokingly, 'Is this a proposal or what?' He laughed nervously and replied, 'No, just mind it for me. And watch out for Free State patrols.'

They had a terrifying journey with sniper fire going on all around them, especially from the roof of Mountjoy prison, but made it safely to Glasnevin cemetery. Harling commandeered a grave in St Paul's, then gave a receipt from his field notepad to the grave-keeper, telling him that he would be paid in full when the republic came into being. The grave was officially registered in Harling's name some years later, after he had made a collection from prominent republicans, including de Valera, to pay for it.

Their journey back was less traumatic because there was a lull in the fighting. Harling escorted Nora into the Fianna headquarters, where she immediately resumed attending to the wounded. He went back to the field. They would not meet again for another two years.

Harling was on the run throughout that whole period. His mother's house at Phibsborough was raided day and night by the Staters until he was finally captured on 3 September 1922. He was interned first at Mountjoy then transferred to Tintown No. 3 camp, where he was in command of Hut 19. He was on hunger strike for twenty-one days before being transferred to Harepark.

After the cessation of hostilities and the release of Fianna Éireann prisoners towards the end of 1923, there evolved a pattern of fresh thinking within the Fianna. Times were changing. There was never a split in the Fianna but one almost came about in February 1924, when a resolution was passed stating that 'Fianna Éireann should not carry arms but confine itself to being only a Boy Scout Training Organisation'. A bitter and irreconcilable difference of opinion erupted between the militant faction, who wanted to copper-fasten their ties with the IRA, and the non-militant faction, who wanted to sever those ties.

Joseph Reynolds, the national secretary of the Fianna, who had been released from prison in August 1923 and promoted to chief scoutmaster of the Dublin Brigade, claimed that it had been his idea to change the Fianna from a militarily orientated organisation to a strictly boy-scout one and that this idea was fully endorsed by the officers who had served with him in the war against the British. In reality, however, he was the bitterest opponent of the changes to the Fianna's constitution.

The Special Intelligence Unit of an garda síochána (the Specials) knew that the sudden turn away from the gun and bomb by Joseph

Reynolds and his friends was a matter of expediency and that in reality they were still active members of the IRA who were playing a prominent role in recruiting young boys from the ranks of the Fianna into the IRA. They wanted to put an end to that activity.

Although the Specials had spies high up in the IRA, they had none in the Fianna and were desperate to recruit someone from the Fianna's ranks. That recruit would obviously have to be a very respected and trusted member, a man beyond reproach, who would yet have no qualms about joining their side. But who was that man? Whom could they target? And how would they go about it?

When Seán Harling was released from prison on 5 February 1924 after signing the declaration of fidelity, he returned to the Dublin Brigade of the Fianna as OC and declared his support for the non-militant faction. But when he turned up at the Dáil secretariat to resume his position as filing clerk, he was told that the minister for finance had ordered his indefinite suspension. The reason given was that he still had not severed his connections with the Irregulars. Harling protested, maintaining that he had never at any time taken advantage of his position as clerk in the secretariat to assist the Irregulars. He spent six months appealing and protesting but his appeals fell on deaf ears. Had the wheels of entrapment been set in motion?

In August 1924 Harling got a job in the Leinster Soap Company. Later that month he met Nora Redican again at a Fianna Éireann function in the Mansion House. They hit it off and she became his fiancée. They were devoted and loyal lovers who soon became the best-known and most-admired couple in the Dartry and Donny-brook areas. They went everywhere and did everything together and could be seen daily walking the streets hand in hand.

As predicted by many, their courtship was a short one, for they could hardly wait to get married and settle into a place of their own – as Nora said, 'away from the confines of Woodpark lodge', where the Redicans were now living. The two were married on 8 December 1925 in the Church of the Holy Name, Rathmines, and secured affordable rented accommodation in a house on the Rathmines Road, where they lived happily and peacefully for a number of months.

But for Harling, even though he had let it be known that he had turned his back on militancy, and for other republican ex-internees, work was hard to come by. They were blacklisted by employers, and those who did give them work often sacked them after a visit from the Specials. That, indeed, was what happened in the Leinster Soap Company for Seán Harling.

While the Specials were harassing republicans out of employment, they were also keeping their eyes and ears open for the emergence of a likely candidate whom they could lure into spying for them. When Seán Harling emerged as that candidate, they swooped swiftly. It seems that someone suggested Harling, telling the Specials that Harling's position in the Fianna was confused since the bitter row had broken out between the militant and non-militant factions.

They knew he was chauffeur to the Countess Markievicz and that she and her fellow officers held him in high esteem. But they also knew that he had been one of the Fianna's best intelligence people and so was in the ideal position of trust. In fact, he was the one person they were sure could furnish them with the information they required without arousing a scintilla of suspicion.

It seems that Eoin O'Duffy, chief of police, gave the go-ahead to David Neligan, head of Special Branch and one of Collins' spies in Dublin Castle, and his deputy Detective Seán O'Connell, to do whatever they thought necessary to force Harling to turn his coat. They in turn selected three special detectives of equal rank to formulate a plan. They were Éamon Broy (another of Collins' spies in the castle and a reputed supporter of de Valera), Superintendent Finian O'Driscoll (who was well known as a nasty piece of work) and a third officer. These men came up with a plan to harass, starve and frighten Harling into working for them.

Every time they took him in they brought him to Pearse Street garda station, perhaps to familiarise him with the milieu. Neligan and O'Connell always threatened to starve him out of the country by making sure he would never find work in his native Dublin so long as he was associating with the Irregulars. The other officers issued threats of a more sinister nature, including telling him how easy it would be for them to spread the word that he was already an informer.

When they realised that their current approach was not working, they changed tactics and intensified their efforts. One day in early May 1926, the Specials arrested three prominent members of the IRA, or so they told Harling, and brought them to the Bridewell garda station for questioning. They picked Harling up at the same time and brought him to Pearse Street, simply 'to frighten the shite out of him', as Neligan once put it.

They did not follow the normal legally required procedure (which exists to this day) of bringing the prisoner over to the desk sergeant to have his name, his address, the names of the arresting officers and the time of arrest entered into the station's log book, and to hand over his effects and the contents of his pockets to be put into a sealed envelope for safe keeping until his release. Instead he was brought straight to a holding cell, where he was grilled, threatened and roughed up for a couple of days by three Specials heavies – one from Pearse Street itself and the other two from Dublin Castle.

The purpose of the terrifying interrogation was, of course, to try and scare Harling into spying on the Fianna. They told him how simple it would be for them to shoot him and dump his body down an alleyway, with his comrades in the IRA taking the blame for it.

'Your name is not entered into the log book, Seán; you have all your possessions; you are not here in Pearse Street and we never picked you up. So officially we know nothing of your where-abouts.'

'The scenario is simple,' one of them continued. 'We paid you a visit; you gave us vital information about three prominent IRA activists, whom we arrested immediately after leaving your house. Your comrades, when they learned it was you who had informed on them – and we will make sure that they do hear it was you – took you out and shot you through the back of the head, then dumped your body. As you are aware, Seán, the matter will go down as just another informer being shot by the IRA. So simple, isn't it? And you know well that we are capable of doing it, don't you, Seán?'

In the meantime, Harling's wife, who was heavily pregnant, and her mother were frantically scouring the town looking for him. Nora had gone into hysterics two days earlier when she had returned from town to find their bed and other items of fur-niture upturned, their clothing scattered around the house and her husband missing. Beside herself with worry, she had dashed down to her mother's house, falling a few times along the way and scraping her nose, knuckles and knees, and fallen in the door, screaming, 'Seán is gone and the house is smashed up!'

After the mother had managed to calm her they had sat down

to a cup of tea and discussed the matter calmly. They had deduced that the Specials must have raided the house and taken Seán in for questioning. They spent the next couple of days searching for him at their local garda stations without success. The mother, now becoming really concerned for his safety, said, 'Okay, Nora, let's go over to the castle and demand to know where they've taken him.'

When the Specials at Dublin Castle told her they had not ordered a raid on her house and had no idea of the whereabouts of her husband, Nora broke down in tears and was consoled by her worried mother. Of course, they did not believe what the Specials had told them, and when they left the castle they headed straight over to the Bridewell. They were told that he was not there either and that no one knew anything about him having been taken into any garda station for questioning. They suggested that the two women try Dublin Castle.

'We've already been to the bloody castle, you bastards,' Nora screamed at them. 'You bloody bastards have him locked away somewhere! I know you have, you bastards!'

The mother threw a consoling arm around her upset daughter once again. She slowly guided her towards the door, saying, 'Come on now, Nora, come on. Don't be letting yourself get so upset. We'll find out where he is. Don't you worry.'

Unbeknown to them a detective – a friendly one as it turned out – was going off duty and had overheard them asking about Harling. He came up behind the two women at the door and deliberately bumped into them. Then, after apologising loudly, he whispered, 'Try Pearse Street,' and hurried on his way.

It was close to midnight when they arrived at Pearse Street station. Nora breathlessly and excitedly demanded that an astonished desk sergeant, who had just come on duty, let her see her husband. The sergeant calmed her down, then said, 'Okay, missus, what's your husband's name then?'

She told him and he beckoned them to sit on the wooden bench beside his desk while he checked the station log for her husband's name. They had hardly sat down on the bench when the sergeant said, 'I'm sorry, missus, but there's no Seán Harling entered here. Maybe he's in the Bridewell.'

'He's not in the bloody Bridewell. He's here and I want to see him!' Nora barked.

'Look, missus,' the sergeant said, coming from behind the desk with the book and showing it to her, 'there's only four prisoners held in this station at the moment and your husband is not one of them. I'm sorry.'

'My husband is here! We know he's here and we're not leaving until we see him and are assured that no harm has come to him!' Nora yelled at the bewildered sergeant.

The sergeant was scratching his head and wondering what he was going to do about this apparently deranged woman when David Neligan walked through the door. He had been informed that two women were looking for Harling. Nora, spotting him, yelled, 'You, Neligan! You lousy bastard! What have you done with my Seán?' then broke down in tears again.

Neligan, displaying no emotion other than a sly grin, ignored her, went over to the desk sergeant and whispered in his ear. The sergeant leaned back and looked at Neligan with a dumbfounded expression on his face. Then he grabbed a bunch of keys, looked over at the two sobbing women, commandingly said, 'Wait there a minute,' then disappeared through a door with Neligan.

Seán Harling had just put his head to the pillow when the

sergeant opened the cell door and entered. He was followed by Neligan, who said threateningly, 'Right, Harling, get dressed. You're wanted downstairs. And look sharp.'

'What do they want from me now?' Harling thought as he struggled to put on his clothes. But the sigh of relief that enveloped him when he saw his wife and mother-in-law sitting on that bench was, he said, indescribable.

'You're free to go now, Seán,' Neligan told him, and with a smirk he added, 'but if I were in your shoes I'd give some very serious thought to that little scenario my officers painted for you last night.'

As he turned towards the door the desk sergeant yelled, 'Hold on, Mr Harling, I can't let you leave without your personal possessions.'

'They were never taken off me,' Harling replied.

The sergeant looked at Neligan suspiciously, probably thinking, 'What were they up to with this prisoner in my station?' Harling emerged from that station a frightened man, but not a broken one. Their tactics had failed.

Two days later the Specials picked him up again and once more brought him to Pearse Street. This time they sat him in a comfortable chair in an office and gave him tea, biscuits and a cigarette. He had been there a good five minutes and was wondering what the bloody hell was going on when in walked two friendly faces from the past – Richard Mulcahy and Diarmuid O'Hegarty, two government officials who knew Harling well and whom Harling respected – and Éamon Broy. Apparently Mulcahy and O'Hegarty had agreed to try and entice Harling into working for the state.

Before they started on him Harling complained to them about the treatment meted out to him by the interrogating officers on his previous visit to that establishment. Mulcahy and O'Hegarty seemed genuinely surprised and shocked to hear about it. They asked Broy what he knew about the allegation, but of course Broy knew nothing. Mulcahy told Broy to take note of the complaint, then tried to gain Harling's trust by assuring him that there would be no repeat of that episode and promising that the officers who had threatened his life would be severely disciplined.

After the initial soft soaping they got down to business, telling him straight that they wanted him to work for the government as an intelligence officer. They reminded him of how well his brother Frank had been doing in the civil service since he had sided with the Free State, and how he could have his own civil-service clerk's position back if he would only help them out.

Broy told Harling that their inside men had given them very reliable information that de Valera was going to break away from Sinn Féin within the next couple of weeks to form a new party. He intended to take his seat and the oath of allegiance in the Dáil if elected. O'Hegarty said that the whole political landscape in Ireland was rapidly changing from one of contention and hatred to one of reconciliation and peace, that the lingering hostilities from the civil war would very soon be at an end and that everything would be the same as it had been before the truce.

Mulcahy told Harling that de Valera could well be the new taoiseach after the next general election and that they would all be working under one of his ministers then.

'It will be like old times, Seán,' he said.

They told him that they greatly admired his courage in taking the anti-militant stance in the Fianna and that they had heard he was still in secret contact with de Valera.

'We remember with affection, Seán, the great work you did

for de Valera when you were his aide during the war of independence. You can do great work for him again by becoming one of our intelligence officers within the Fianna. You will have money in your pocket to put bread and butter on the table for yourself and your wife again. Of course, Seán, you know you will need to have a steady income when the baby is born.' They even offered him some money there and then, but he refused to take it.

Harling asked if they had finished their business with him. Broy answered, 'Yes, for the time being, Seán.' He stood up and told them there was no way he was going to join them, no matter what inducements they laid before him. As he was walking out the door, Broy shouted after him menacingly, 'Oh, by the way, Seán, we've released the three IRA men we picked up the other day', reminding him in of the alternative they had put to him four days ago.

Harling took what they were telling him about the coming changes to mean that if he joined them now and used his trusted position in the Fianna to spy on certain members who, they told him, as if he did not know, were still recruiting young boys into the IRA, he would be helping to hasten those changes.

As he strolled home he pondered who could have put them on to him. Who could have given them the information about his supposed contact with de Valera and his anti-militant stance? Did they already have a spy in the Fianna? And if they did, what information did they want that they couldn't get from him?

Domestically, things were going from bad to worse for Harling. His financial situation had further declined. Food was scarce, the rent on his apartment was a few weeks in arrears and, to top it all, his first child was due to be born in August. So, out of sheer desperation, swallowing his pride, he wrote the following letter to Diarmuid O'Hegarty on 3 June 1926:

To D. O. Hegarty Esq.

A Chara,

When I was employed as a Messenger in the Secretariat of the Dáil from Oct. 1918, to June 1922, no Unemployment Card was stamped for me. I am now out of work for 6 months and if I had those stamps on my Card I would be entitled to benefit. I shall be much obliged if you will have the arrears paid for that period so that I may be in benefit, as I am at the moment very badly off.

Mise le Meas
Seán Harling

He had made the serious error of putting down the wrong date, October 1918. The Dáil had not come into being until January 1919. When the Specials were shown the letter they were delighted about the mistake, and their delight was doubled by the written confirmation of Harling's financial circumstances. They used the error to deny him the right to draw the unemployment benefit to which he claimed he was entitled. They were sure now that they had their man and gleefully turned the screws, making his daily life a total misery with harassment and pressure. Still, however, he held fast.

Seán Harling and his wife were soon forced, by dire need, to leave their rented accommodation and move in with the Redicans, whose circumstances was somewhat better than their own. The father was employed as a gardener by the owners of Woodpark estate, the Thompsons, and he had been given the gate lodge rent free as part of his wages. The two younger brothers, Patrick and Laurence, were in apprenticeship to different trades. Tom got casual work now and then, and James, unemployable because of his war wounds, was contributing a few bob to the weekly household budget by other means. That combined weekly income was sufficient to keep the Redicans' heads above water.

Now, however, they had two more mouths to feed, no extra money coming in and none likely to come in for the foreseeable future, especially with Harling blacklisted in Dublin. This new circumstance put the Redicans under tremendous pressure. With a baby arriving soon God only knew how they would cope.

Harling was highly respected and trusted by the Fianna. The countess would give him one of her cars for his own private use whenever he requested it. She also befriended the Redicans and employed Thomas as one of her chauffeurs, and Laurence, an apprentice mechanic, often serviced her cars. However, the Fianna did nothing to help Harling through that terrible period of deprivation in his life. Perhaps they were unable to because so many were in the same position.

Chapter 6

The Redicans Continued

The very day the Redican brothers and Thomas Weymes arrived in Mountjoy from Beggar's Bush they went on hunger strike in protest. On the twelfth day of the hunger strike, A. W. Cope, acting on behalf of the minister for home affairs, instructed the governor to remove the three men from the prison hospital to Dr Steevens' hospital to recover their health, so that they would be fit to attend an inquiry that was being set up into their case. They were placed under heavy guard there.

The men responded well to their treatment and were fully recovered after a fortnight. The medical staff told them that they were well enough to return to Mountjoy, but they refused to cooperate and malingered in hospital for another twenty-three days. The hospital management got fed up and complained about them to the Ministry of Home Affairs. The Ministry of Home Affairs, in turn, wrote to the chief commissioner of Dublin Metropolitan Police on 4 May, instructing him to take the Redican brothers back into the custody of the governor of Mountjoy. The next day, the brothers were taken back to prison and immediately resumed their hunger strike.

Five days into their second strike the governor informed them that a date for the hearing of their appeal in the Dublin Court of Conscience had been fixed. They called the strike off.

In order to give the Redicans and Thomas Weymes a fair hearing, the minister for home affairs sent a representative of the provisional government to meet with a representative of the Irregulars to verify whether the IRA had sanctioned the 1921 bank raids. The representative came back with a statement saying that the bank raids were never authorised and that the IRA had not received one shilling of the proceeds.

On 16 May 1922 the governor of Mountjoy received an order from Oriel House, Westland Row, to have the Redican brothers ready to be escorted by Sergeant Halpin to the Court of Conscience, South William Street, for their trial the next day at 11 a.m.

Judges Creed Meredith and Arthur Clery presided. And when the hearing was over the two men were sent back to prison as remand prisoners to await the findings of the court. They were happy with this because remand prisoners had it much easier in jail than convicted ones. They were allowed more visits from family and friends and to smoke without asking permission but, most importantly, they were allowed to wear their own clothes.

The brothers were fully confident that they would win the appeal, but they were to be disappointed because in the meantime civil war broke out. Now, even if the court directed that they be released, no way was the provisional government going to free two hardened and experienced gunmen from custody, knowing full well that they would fight with the Irregulars. The brothers and Thomas Weymes had declared their support for the anti-Treaty side before being unceremoniously bundled back to Mountjoy.

Then, on 25 August, two months into the civil war and after one of the judges, Arthur Clery, had sided with the republicans, the brothers were dealt a devastating blow. The secretary of the Ministry of Home Affairs sent a directive to the governor of Mountjoy:

Governor,

Will you please have the following communicated to the brothers J. J. and T. Redican, at present detained in Mountjoy Prison?

The members of the court appointed to inquire as to the justice of the retention in custody of Messrs James J. Redican and Thomas Redican convicted of robbery by a British court-martial on 12/5/21 have now reported to The Minister for Home Affairs.

Neither judge has found that there was any miscarriage of justice in the conviction of the said prisoners or that they should now be released.

Both judges have, however, reported that the sentences imposed by the court-martial were unnecessarily severe and have recommended that the Government should exercise its clemency by remitting part of the unexpired portion of these sentences. The Government will take this recommendation into consideration at the end of three months, but in view of the circumstances of the country it does not feel justified at present in announcing the granting of any remission of sentence to men who have been convicted of bank robbery.

Ernest Blythe,
Acting Minister for Home Affairs

The governor read the message to the brothers on 28 August. They were on the verge of threatening hunger strike when the governor told them that he would leave them on the remand wing until further notice. The Redicans were content to accept that situation and during the time they spent on the remand wing they openly fraternised with Irregular internees. After four months the governor received a phone call from general headquarters enquiring about the Redicans' prison status. Word had reached them that someone inside the prison was receiving and delivering messages for IRA prisoners, and they suspected the Redicans as being the culprits.

From July 1922 until as late as October 1923, James Redican was 'doing centre' (that is, acting as the secret channel for all communications between military prisoners and their friends outside) for republicans in Mountjoy prison. He was able to do this through visits from his mother and sister. They were eventually caught, too, however, and were barred from visiting the prison for a couple of months.

In December a letter arrived at the prison from the office of the adjutant general:

General Head Quarters
Beggar's Bush Barracks
Dublin.

To Governor M.J.

Confirming phone call of date you will now receive the Redican Brothers into proper custody for completion of sentence or until receipt of further instructions.

Seán O'Connell

On 31 December, the brothers were transferred from the remand wing to the convict wing, but the governor allowed them to continue wearing their own clothes. They immediately went on hunger strike and remained on hunger strike until 13 January 1923, when they decided to change tactics in favour of a campaign of disobedience. Despite this period of rebellion in the prison, the Redicans' mother and sister had their visiting rights restored and resumed smuggling messages from IRA prisoners to their people outside.

The Redicans were proving to be the toughest and most troublesome prisoners that the governor and warders of Mountjoy civil prison ever had to deal with. The governor held a conference with his senior officers to try and work out an effective strategy to deal with them. They decided to ask the prison chaplain to talk to them about their behaviour.

In the middle of May 1923, the chaplain had a heart-to-heart chat with James about the brothers' disruptive conduct in the prison and appealed to him and Thomas to accept the findings of the Appeals Court and get on with their sentence in peace and harmony with the governor and prison staff. James Redican was not due for release until 11 May 1936, but with the remission of his sentence for good behaviour he could be released on 1 October 1932. Thomas was not due for release until 11 May 1933, but the earliest possible date of his release on remission was 7 July 1930.

James Redican told the chaplain that the version of the Court of Conscience's findings Ernest Blythe had given to the governor was not the true one. He gave his own version to the chaplain, who sent it to the Ministry of Home Affairs as a petition on their behalf:

Sir,

James Redican has told me that while they were recovering in Dr Steven's [*sic*] Hospital after having been released on hunger strike to there; the Provisional Government offered him an inquiry into their case. He gladly accepted that inquiry. But, the inquiry was never finished, he said, because the burning of the Four Courts came on and Mr Arthur Clery went with the Irregulars and Mr Creed Meredith remained with the state. And that it is on record that Mr Clery had recommended their release.

Considering the fact of their being sentenced by British court-marshal [*sic*] of extreme annoyance it is within your power to show clemency now and give them that mitigation of sentence which you held out to them earlier. I venture to suggest that you be good enough to bring my proposal to the M.O.H.A.

The governor received a response to the prison chaplain's petition from the secretary to the minister for home affairs on behalf of the minister on 29 May:

> It will be remembered that J. and T. Redican were convicted of robbery by a British court-martial on 12/5/1921: that the Free State Government appointed a court to consider the justice of the conviction and that this board was informed by the acting Minister on the 28/8/1922 that the court had not found that there was a miscarriage of justice in the prisoner's conviction or that there was a case for their release.
>
> I am to add that these prisoners are notoriously insubordinate and they must be brought to realise that they are not imprisoned at public expense for their amusement. Their conduct in prison has been unsatisfactory and the Minister for Home Affairs is not disposed to consider the question of a mitigation of the sentence at present.

On 30 May, the Redicans' mother and sister were granted a visit but were once again caught smuggling out messages for the IRA. They were barred from visiting the prison again for several months.

The next day the brothers, bitterly disappointed with the response from the Ministry of Home Affairs to the prison chaplain's petition, went on hunger and thirst strike for the first time.

The medical officer's report to the governor on 11 June 1923 read:

> The Governor,
>
> In accordance with rule 172(5), I have to report that I am of opinion that the Redican Brothers on Hunger strike today the 11th are going down hill rapidly owning to their depriving themselves of liquid entirely in the case of J. J. Redican and partially in his brother's case. They have now reached the stage when a collapse is to be expected and they are unlikely to survive their

sentences unless they resume taking food. I am reporting them in accordance with the usual routine in such cases on this date.

11/6/23
B. J. Hackett Med. O.

Two days later, the medical officer reported to the governor:

James Redican's tongue is shrunken and dry, pulse feeble and temperature 96.6. I apprehend danger point is at hand in this case. Thomas Redican is weak. He complains of pains everywhere. Tongue coated and dry, pulse 60 and weak, temperature 97. Mattress must be changed immediately. I apprehend that the danger point is at hand in this case. 9.30 a.m.

(Sg) B. J. Hackett MO

The prison chaplain, very concerned about the brothers' welfare, coaxed them off their hunger strike by promising to do all in his power to have their case reviewed. When he promised to petition the minister for home affairs again on their behalf, James Redican explained some more details to him. True to his word, the prison chaplain sent the petition to the minister on 26 June:

James Redican does not dispute the facts brought against him regarding the raids on 5 October and 16 November 1920 but denies any participation in the raid of 7 February 1921 [the one that got them convicted in the first place].

His contention is: (1) He was tried by British court-martial at a time that [when] these courts were considered illegal by those now in charge of Government. (2) His raids were conducted under orders from Brigadier David [T. J.] Burke, his superior officer who is a jeweller in Mullingar. And he claims that he can produce credible witnesses to prove that the raids were official.

He also believes that some game of trickery went on somewhere by someone to keep them in prison because, he said, he

later learned that the British authorities had ordered their release with all other Sinn Féin prisoners. But upon their release
they were re-arrested, this time by armed men who said they
were IRA. They hunger struck while in their hands and were
transferred to Mountjoy prison.

I trust that this letter will be past [sic] on to the appropriate
authority.

The brothers had been going on and off hunger strike between 25 September 1922 and 6 August 1923. During those
eleven months of striking, protesting, non-compliance with
prison regulations and petitioning the minister for home affairs, James Redican still managed to 'do centre' for the IRA
prisoners.

When the General Prisons Board for Ireland learned that the
Redicans were still wearing their own clothes they strongly re-
buked the governor and ordered him to strip the brothers of their
clothes immediately, to force them to wear convict clothes and to
punish them for insubordination.

The brothers had only come off their latest hunger strike two
days earlier, 6 August, and were recuperating in the prison hospital.
The governor did not want to punish them while they were in a
delicate state of health. But twenty-three days later, the medical
officer certified to the governor that the brothers were now fit for
punishment.

They knew that they were being prepared for punishment and
were ready for the warders, led by Davis and Crowley, when they
entered the cell the next day at 6 a.m. and ordered them up. The
Redicans refused to get out of their beds. The warders dragged
them from their cells to the tower, where they tried to force them
to put on prison garb. The Redicans punched Crowley and Davis
out the door onto the landing, but after a long, rough struggle a

dozen warders managed to restrain them with handcuffs. They stripped the brothers naked and dressed them in prison clothes.

In protest, the brothers went on hunger strike. This one was to be the longest and most life-threatening of all the strikes they had undertaken. They were determined to be recognised as political prisoners.

In the meantime, their mother, who had seen and heard nothing about them since her last visit in June, wrote to the governor enquiring about her sons' health. She received no reply, and wrote again on 9 August asking the governor 'for God Almighty Sake' to let her know if her two sons were dead or alive. She enclosed a stamped addressed envelope for a reply which she did not receive.

After the Prisons Board in Dublin Castle heard about the pleas from the mother to the governor of Mountjoy for information about the health of her sons, they sent him a note on 11 August:

> Governor, you may send this woman a short letter after consultation with the M.O. informing her as to the present state of her sons' health.

Einni O'Frigil

On 24 September (about three months after the civil war had ended and at a time when the government was about to draw up plans for the release of republican prisoners) the assistant secretary of the Ministry of Home Affairs phoned Mountjoy and told them to 'instruct the governor to inform the Redicans that if they conform to the prison regulations the minister will be prepared to consider a mitigation of their sentences'. He added that 'on no account will they effect their release by any hunger striking or other insubordinate methods'.

The governor optimistically read the message to the brothers that same day. But he was bitterly disappointed with their response. Thomas replied, 'I don't want to hear any more about it. I am not coming off hunger strike.' And James replied, 'You can send that back to them. We are here in illegal custody.'

The prison chaplain, having consulted with the Redicans, wrote to the assistant secretary of the Ministry of Home Affairs:

Mitigation,

I take it in the sense of shortening their sentences [and the] duration of their imprisonment? Would it be possible to have the term mitigation applied rather to their status as prisoners than to the term of their sentence? The two have assured me that if the stigma of being convicts were removed from them they would willingly submit to the prison regulations (and what subsequent provision might be made as to their being made 'ticket of leave' men). I venture to suggest that you be good enough to bring my proposal before the Minister of Home Affairs.

The chaplain, apparently, did not receive a reply from the ministry.

Thirty days into their latest hunger strike the brothers were going in and out of consciousness. Their mother and sister were granted a visit and were shocked to see the state they were in. But because they were speaking in low tones the warders removed them from the prison once again.

On 3 October, their mother, not having been allowed visit her sons for some time, was convinced that they were dead and that the governor was hiding that fact from her. Sick with worry, she wrote once more to the governor for information about them:

34 Oxford Road Ranelagh Dublin.
To Governor Mountjoy Civil Prison.

Mr Faulkner,

As you are aware on last visiting my two sons under your care in Mountjoy Civil Prison Thomas, the younger and innocent prisoner, was unconscious and James was semiconscious.

I ask you now would you not think that I, as their mother, would like to know are they dead or alive? I am commencing to think that we are turning into one of those Muhammadan Countries where there is no civilisation. Or what is Saintly Ireland turning to at all? When two boys innocent of their charges are isolated away in prison in agony of death as they were when I last visited them. The poor creatures, I am sure, cannot but be alive as poor skeletons or rather the breath only barely being in them. Oh God! Are you, Mr Faulkner, a father? If so, you should think of a mother's feelings for her children. I ask you now on this occasion as before, for the love and honour of God, let me know, are my two sons dead or alive?

What is wrong at all? Are you keeping their deaths, if they are dead, a secret from me their mother? Please let me visit them.

An answer at your earliest convenience would be appreciated. I enclose a stamped addressed envelope for your reply.

I am, Mr Faulkner, the mother of the dying boys, James and Thomas Redican.

Early on the morning of 12 October, not having received a reply to her letter, the mother and Nora arrived at the gates of Mountjoy to enquire about the welfare of the brothers. The medical officer came out and spoke to them and then gave his written report to the governor: 'The Redican Brothers are very much weaker this morning and are fading fast. Their mother has been informed of their condition.'

The governor decided under the circumstances to grant them a visit. He sent Principal Warder Robert Grace out to escort them into the prison and Grace warned them that their visit would be aborted immediately if they began whispering. He said that if James and Thomas were too weak to talk loudly enough for Mr Downes (the officer overseeing the visit) to hear, he would convey the brothers' words to the visitors. The pair gave no response.

When they entered James' cell the mother knelt down and kissed him several times on the cheek, then beckoned to Nora to do the same. When Nora knelt down to kiss her brother he began whispering to her and she whispered back. Mr Downes told them they must speak in a loud tone, but they ignored him and continued whispering. Mr Downes responded by aborting the visit. As he was pushing them out of the cell, the mother remonstrating with him about the dreadful way they were being treated, James shouted, 'Refuse any more of these visits, Nora!'

'We will, James!' she replied.

Later that evening, still very worried about their condition, Nora handed in her letter at the gate addressed to the governor:

> Governor, my two brothers, J. J. and T. C. Redican are on hunger strike in your prison this 45 clear days. Today I called to the prison gates to find out how they were and I was told to visit them. That I did. And I found them to be on their last legs. But because they could not shout out loud enough for the warder to hear them, and the poor things not able to speak, I was pushed out of the cell. So there was no visit allowed. Now, if you please, will you let me know what is all this for? The two are on their last legs.

The governor ordered Robert Grace to bring her to his office, where he explained the situation to her. Then he wrote in his report:

> I saw Miss Redican and explained the Visiting Committee's orders that she failed to conform to the Prison Regulations by not speak-

ing loudly enough to enable the Prison Officer in charge to hear her conversation.

Governor 12/10/23

The Mountjoy prison chaplain, M. S. MacMahon, who had returned from a fortnight's holiday that day, was shocked at the sight of the brothers and became extremely worried about their state of health. He spent the whole night with them, coaxing them into giving up their hunger strike, which they did.

Six days later, after observing closely the continued tension between the Redicans and the prison staff, even though the brothers were extremely weak, his concern grew for the welfare of the brothers and the safety of prison officers. He wrote a letter to the vice-chairman of the Prisons Board:

Holy Cross College
Clonliffe
18/10/23

My Dear Vice-Chairman,

Since my return from holidays I have kept in close touch with the Redican Brothers who are proving such a source of anxiety and trouble to all the officers who have to deal with them. They are determined and difficult men. Even the most experienced Prison Officers find them very difficult to handle. And in order to avoid a tragedy in the prison I would venture to ask you to put my view before the responsible authority.

In response to the chaplain's letter the brothers were sent to Dr Steevens' hospital, where they spent twelve days recovering from the effects of their hunger strike before being sent back to the prison hospital.

For the next couple of months the brothers continued with their campaign of disobedience until the Mountjoy staff could no longer cope with them. The Prisons Board decided that the staff in Portlaoise prison would be better able to handle them. They were transferred there in February 1924.

On arrival at Portlaoise the brothers were greeted by the governor, Mr Blake – whom they recognised as having been governor of Mountjoy when they had first gone there having being sentenced in 1921 – and four burly, intimidating-looking warders. But of course nothing and nobody intimidated the Redican brothers. They decided to test the mettle of the governor and his staff by beginning a campaign of disobedience.

In the middle of March, however, realising that their current form of protest was not having the desired effect, they decided to intensify their quest for political status by stripping naked and going on hunger strike. Within a week of this hunger strike's beginning, the governor managed to persuade them to rethink their tactics, convincing them that granting political status was not in his power. They would be better off abandoning the strike and trying to petition the minister for home affairs once more. They took the governor's advice:

Petition written on 26 March 1924 by James Redican for submission to the Minister for Home Affairs:

A Cara,
I write this concerning a petition which I sent to you when in Mountjoy 6–7 weeks ago, in which I referred to case, and a request re smoking.
  Now sir, if smoking is refused to me it is my intention to continue strike. I am entitled to the treatment granted to myself, my

brother and Thomas Weymes, by British authorities. And it was the gentleman who acts as governor here who was instructed to grant us that treatment.

I am even denied the Rights and Concessions given to English Convicts in English Convict Prisons although I am a British Prisoner. Captured and tried by British Military Forces. And I am detained here under a British Committal order – namely the Restoration of order in Ireland Regulations Act. As a prisoner of war with England I am entitled to be treated as such. And failing that I am at least entitled to treatment as an English Convict.

Hoping for satisfactory reply – if not I will continue strike.

Is mise le meas mor
Seamus S. Ó Roideacháin

The General Prisons Board was frothing at the mouth with anger when they read Redican's latest petition. They were determined not to let the minister for home affairs read this one. They wrote a stinging letter to the governor of Portlaoise prison:

Portlaoighise Prison
26-3-24.

SUBJECT – IMPROPER MEMORIAL WRITTEN BY CONVICT JAMES J. REDICAN
E571. –Authority requested not to submit it.

Governor/Inform this convict that you will not in future accept any insolent communications and that you have suppressed this one. Have him punished. This is a notorious bank robber and he should be sternly handled at the outset or otherwise he will give you no end of annoyances.

He should not be permitted in any interview with you to indulge in any such rigmaroles and he should be given no opportunity to emit this rancorous steam with which he appears to be superabundantly inflated.

The governor replied:

Chairman,

Convict informed as above and gravely warned that any attempt at repetition of an offence of this nature will be severely punished.

For his present offence I awarded 3 days No. 1 P. D. in C. C. and forfeit 7 days remission - the petition suppressed.

L. J. Blake, Governor
29/3/24

The brothers ended the strike three days later in favour of their campaign of disobedience.

Out of the blue three months later, on 20 June, the governor of Portlaoise prison received a letter from Einnie Ó Frigil, saying that 'The Governor General on the advice of the Minister for Justice has been pleased to order that the said James J. and Thomas C. Redican be released on licence.'

On 2 July 1924, the Redicans were freed on licence with their movements restricted to the Dublin area and under the condition that they report to their local garda station once a week. They were known to the gardaí as ticket-of-leave men. Their release and that of Thomas Weymes came at the same time as the release of the last batch of IRA prisoners interned since the beginning of the civil war.

When they arrived home in Dublin they were not only greeted by their delighted parents and siblings but also by some ex-republican internees and their families, who wished to show their appreciation to James for 'doing centre' for them in Mountjoy.

There was a story in circulation in the Redican family – which may be just a story – that one evening at the height of the civil war the mother paid a visit to the house of a woman she was friendly with on the Ranelagh Road, whose husband was sympathetic to the republican cause. Mr Arthur Clery, one of the judges at the brothers' trial, happened to be there at the time. She confronted him with the question, 'Why did you recommend my sons' continued incarceration?'

Clery replied, quite bluntly, 'I recommended their release, madam, but I knew that that wouldn't happen during the civil war because of their anti-Treaty stance. However, I expected that they would be treated as interned prisoners.'

The mother related the encounter with Mr Arthur Clery to her son James on one of her visits to the prison. That, perhaps, was how James was able to give a different version of the outcome of the Court of Appeal's decision from the one Ernest Blythe related to the prison chaplain. It seems, however, that before the mother told the brothers about her meeting with Arthur Clery James received a smuggled message from an IRA officer telling him the same story.

The Redican brothers and Thomas Weymes were in no doubt that they were deliberately kept in prison until the end of the civil war because they were classed by the authorities as republican prisoners, even though they were not officially given that status. Also, it seems, those men who were considered by the state to be the most dangerous republicans were the last to be released.

Chapter 7

De Valera's Quest for Power

In August 1923, Sinn Féin contested the general election and won forty-four seats. But because they were still an abstentionist party, they did not take them. De Valera worked stealthily over the next three years to change that policy.

Throughout the year of 1925 there were murmurs of dissatisfaction within the ranks of the republican movement about de Valera's apparent march in the direction of Dáil Éireann, which was not what the IRA had envisaged. They feared that he was 'going wrong' and, in December that year, they withdrew their allegiance from him.

> You'll hear it on the mountain.
> You'll hear it in the glen.
> You'll hear it in the valley,
> The tramp of marching men.
> God give you strength and bearing.
> God give you strength and daring
> To blow up Dáil Éireann,
> You Irish volunteers.

Then on 9 March 1926, at a special Sinn Féin *ardfheis*, Éamon de Valera nailed his colours to the mast. He proposed a campaign to remove the oath of allegiance so that republicans could take their seats in both the Dáil and the Seanad. It was becoming clearer to the republicans that did not trust de Valera that he was indeed, as they saw it, 'going wrong'.

On 16 May 1926, in La Scala theatre on Prince's Street, off Dublin's O'Connell Street, de Valera and Frank Aiken, whom the IRA had deposed as their chief of staff only six months earlier, split from Sinn Féin and launched their new republican party, Fianna Fáil (Warriors of Destiny). A huge percentage of IRA volunteers from all over the twenty-six counties joined their local *cumann*. What had changed their mind about de Valera in such a short time? Why did they join a party that had further split the republican movement and whose leader had not earlier enjoyed their support?

A month after the forming of Fianna Fáil, 'de Valera's man' Seán Harling, although still a member of the Fianna Éireann, joined the Special Intelligence Unit of an garda síochána. Before joining, however, he laid down definite conditions. He made it clear to them, and in particular to his handler David Neligan, that under no circumstances would he betray any of his old companions or any gains they had made before June 1926. They accepted his conditions. He was sworn in and a job was secured for him in Barden's garage in Ranelagh as cover for the sudden upturn in his fortunes. He moved back to the apartment on the Rathmines Road. Harling reported to Pearse Street, a garda station he knew too well.

But why the sudden change of heart? Had Harling been waiting for the split and then the go-ahead from some person or persons within the new Fianna Fáil/IRA before he could join the Free State secret service? Or was he just starved into it?

The Specials were satisfied with his work at first. There was a marked increase in their intelligence on the covert nature of Fianna Éireann. They gained information on the secret monthly meetings of Fianna militants where no minutes were kept. They learned the unwritten principles that formed part of their constitution, such as backing up the IRA by gathering intelligence, caretaking arms dumps and couriering messages. They found out that the Fianna still sent delegates to confer with the IRA on operational matters, two of them being William Roe and T. J. Ryan, and that Joseph Reynolds, the national secretary and chief scoutmaster in Dublin, supposedly a non-militant, acted as liaison officer between them. They gathered the names and addresses of young militants who were soon to be initiated into the IRA.

One such boy, young William Cusack of 22 Eccles Street, Dublin, was arrested in August 1926 while in possession of firearms and a bomb. He claimed that he did not know what was in the parcel or what he was to do with it. Because of his youth the court was lenient towards him and put him on probation.

The boy was court-martialled and expelled from the Fianna, but that was merely a ploy designed to fool the Specials into believing that the Fianna no longer tolerated militants. The court martial was chaired by Joseph Reynolds who, almost immediately after expelling young William Cusack, initiated him into the IRA.

The sudden and aggressive monitoring of the Fianna by the Specials severely curtailed their militant activity in the Dublin area. The Fianna leadership became seriously frustrated, realising they had an informer within their ranks. They theorised that it had to be a member who had not been around during the war of independence and the civil war. But who was it?

They called in IRA intelligence to help ferret out the mole. The IRA disagreed with the Fianna theory and told them that the mole had to be someone who was held in high esteem in the Fianna and the republican family. Harling was beyond suspicion, of course. He was not even considered.

Three organisations – Fianna Fáil, the IRA and Fianna Éireann – were involved in the hunt for the mole and they worked together to try and root him out. It was a very frustrating period for them, but a lead to his identity was shortly to loom on the horizon.

In the meantime, in early September 1926, an amendment was inserted into the Fianna Éireann constitution:

> The use of firearms throughout the organisation is strictly forbidden, and no officer or member of Fianna Éireann shall teach the use of same or deliver lectures regarding the usages of same. The aims of the Fianna should be the teaching of Irish history, language, culture and scouting.

This was a step too far for the real militants, who wanted to retain revolver practice. All of them, including Joseph Reynolds and Timothy Coughlan, immediately left the Fianna and joined the Fianna Fáil organisation; Coughlan joined the Con Colbert *cumann* in Dublin's Inchicore.

Towards the end of that month, Seán Harling and an elderly republican named Healy raided a munitions store and got away with a small quantity of ammunition. They brought the cache to a dump known only to Healy. Healy had intended to let a couple of weeks go by before having the IRA shift it to an official army dump, but when he went to check on it one day the Specials were waiting. They retrieved the arms and he was sentenced to nine months in Mountjoy . Harling, of course, was not touched.

When a friend of Healy's visited him in prison Healy told him that it could only have been Seán Harling who had informed on him. Only he and Harling had known where the ammunition was dumped.

When word spread that Harling had been named as the one who had shopped Healy his comrades were dumbfounded. And when questioned by his peers about the allegation, Harling denied any knowledge of the affair, dismissing the accusation as a vicious mischievous lie by someone who was out to tarnish his good name.

At the same time Harling was caretaker of a sizeable arms dump for the Fourth Battalion, Dublin Brigade of the IRA. He knew his peers were aware of this and used it to throw them off the scent and prove his loyalty to the movement. He told them that if he were a spy he could well have netted bigger and better fish for the police with bigger and better dumps than Healy's few bullets. They believed him. After all, he was chauffeur and confidant to their beloved Countess Markievicz. They thanked him for his cooperation and told him the air had been cleared.

To further throw them off the trail he sent a note to the IRA brigade quartermaster asking him to come and shift the dump he was caretaking for him. He added that in the present climate of suspicion it would be prudent if he himself were not informed of the whereabouts of the new dump. The quartermaster agreed and shifted the dump. Harling, it appears, was holding true to his word about not betraying gains already made by the movement before he joined the secret service.

After the Healy debacle the Specials were smarting, realising perhaps that raiding dumps containing small amounts of hardware was less important than capturing the unknown militants who were being trained to use that hardware against them. Policemen at that time were being ambushed and shot the length and breadth of the country by IRA volunteers. Indeed, the reason they had hired Harling in the first place was to root out these new militants.

In the meantime, the government, led by the Cumann na nGaedheal party – which had been formed in January 1923 after splitting from Sinn Féin – had fallen foul of the electorate. With the economy in a mess and massive unemployment throughout the land, they had incurred the wrath of the people.

With a general election due to take place in June 1927, the Cosgrave administration appeared to be sitting back, seemingly taking the people for granted. De Valera's Fianna Fáil, on the other hand, were out and about in the towns and villages, at cross-roads and in the countryside, busily wooing them.

On 25 February 1927, de Valera, accompanied by his aide Frank Gallagher, set sail on the SS *Republic* on a coast-to-coast fund-raising tour of America. The money collected would be used to finance their campaign in the forthcoming general election and to fund the setting up of Fianna Fáil's own national newspaper. The tour was a great success both politically and financially.

Despite not decommissioning their weapons having become a constitutional political party, and being suspected of running illegal training camps for their secret army, Fianna Fáil were growing in popularity with the common people of the state. This increasing popularity gave de Valera the confidence to field eighty-seven candidates in the general election of 9 June 1927. Austin Stack's Sinn Féin put forward fifteen candidates but only managed to win five seats. Fianna Fáil won forty-four, only three fewer than Cosgrave's Cumann na nGaedheal, which lost eleven seats. It was said by most political observers of the day that thousands voted for Fianna Fáil in the belief that they would take their seats if elected.

Fianna Fáil adopted a go-it-alone policy, with de Valera believing he could gain power in the Free State Dáil without the support of any other party. Before he could enter that establishment, however, he would first have to take the oath of allegiance to the British crown – something he could not be seen to do.

Seven days after the election he had a letter published in *The Nation*, a weekly review:

> In view of the attempts to mislead the public and make it appear that republican deputies will ultimately weaken and be got to take the oath of allegiance to the King of England, I want it to be known definitely and finally that under no circumstances whatever will Fianna Fáil deputies take any such oath.
>
> We give allegiance to the Irish nation and the Irish people only, and will never acknowledge allegiance to any other.
>
> We mean to keep our election pledge. The people will see to it that the imposition of the degrading penal oath whereby it is sought to disfranchise one-third of the electorate will be brought quickly to an end.

On the same day de Valera released the above statement, 16 June, Volunteer Healy was released from prison. The next day Harling wrote to him, telling him how glad he was to hear that he was at last free from his long term in prison:

> Well, Mr Healy, I don't know what you are thinking now since you came out, or if you have found out the truth, which I hope you have, or will soon. As for me I am not caring what may be said, as better than me was blamed in the wrong and the truth will come to light some day. If my accuser is telling a lie, I will expect a reply to this letter, and all will be well. Thanking you in anticipation of an early reply.
>
> Yours as always,
> Seán Harling
>
> P. S. Please excuse pencil as no insult intended. S.

Healy never replied.

Harling also wrote to Seán Russell, later to become chief of staff of the IRA, explaining his position, but Russell did not reply either. He apparently believed Healy's side of the story.

De Valera had devised a clever plan to get around taking the oath of allegiance. The first step was to show the electorate that he and his party would take their seats but would not take the oath.

On Thursday, 23 June 1927, de Valera put on a headline-grabbing show when he and the other forty-three elected Fianna Fáil deputies assembled outside the locked gates of Leinster House. They pretended they wanted to go in, knowing quite well they would not be allowed to unless they signed Article 17 of the Treaty. Thousands of Fianna Fáil supporters turned out to cheer them on, but more important to de Valera was the multitude of press reporters and photographers who turned up to witness his performance.

He handed a legal document prepared by three constitutional lawyers, who were members of his party, to the clerk of the Dáil, Colm Ó Murchadha, which stated that the Fianna Fáil deputies could not be excluded from the Dáil because they refused to take the oath. But Ó Murchadha did not want to know about it. The only document he wanted to see in de Valera's hand was Article 17, the one containing the oath of allegiance to the British crown.

When de Valera had presented the document, he turned and walked triumphantly back through the cheering crowds, smiling broadly for the cameras and answering reporters' questions. That day's charade would make prominent headlines in the next day's newspapers throughout the nation and further afield. De Valera had now shown the people of Ireland that he was willing to take his seat.

The second part of his clever plan was to nominate Seán Lemass and Seán T. Ó Ceallaigh as plaintiffs in a writ against the attorney general and two other officers of the Dáil. The writ was presented to the court on 4 July. The idea was to get the court to rule that the exclusion of Fianna Fáil from Dáil Éireann was illegal.

If that failed, the third part of his plan – the sting in the tail – would have to be deployed. Fianna Fáil's National Executive would start a nationwide campaign for a referendum on the oath. When that was up and running, de Valera would invoke Article 48 of the constitution, under which a citizen who could secure 75,000 electors' signatures (of which no more than 15,000 could be from any one constituency) and present them to the government would win the right to a referendum on the question.

Finding 75,000 signatories, of course, would prove no problem for de Valera. He was on to a winner, for he knew that very few Irish citizens would vote to retain allegiance to the king of England. Unless something serious happened to scupper his plan, Éamon de Valera would soon be able to realise his alleged ambition of becoming president of the Free State Dáil, without compromising his republican principles by signing the hated oath of allegiance.

But alas, something serious did happen. On the morning of Sunday, 10 July 1927, a beautiful, sunny, summer's morning, the young Free State justice minister Kevin O'Higgins slipped out of his home, Dunamase, in Blackrock, unbeknown to his bodyguard. He was making his way to twelve o'clock mass in Booterstown when he was ambushed by three assassins, who gunned him down at point-blank range.

At the time nobody knew who had carried out the assassination, and responsibility was never claimed by any organisation or individual. But deliberate rumours, it seemed, were put about by unknown sources. One rumour had it that it was an opportunist killing by three armed republicans, acting unofficially, but undoubtedly with 'liberty of action'. Liberty of action was the principle that armed volunteers who happened upon what they termed a 'legitimate target' could kill him or her without seeking permission from general headquarters. Another rumour had it that the killing was carried out by a number of aggrieved army officers who had been severely disciplined by O'Higgins after a failed mutiny back in March 1924. Yet another rumour put it down to a private vendetta.

According to Terence de Vere White, however, in his book *Kevin O'Higgins* (1948), all the evidence collected by the police at the time told the story of a well-planned and skilfully carried-out ambush:

> The household had gone to church earlier in the morning, and O'Higgins went off by himself to twelve o'clock Mass at Booterstown. At the corner, where Booterstown Avenue meets Cross Avenue, there was a seat, and Mrs O'Higgins, on her way home from an earlier Mass, noticed, without attaching any significance to the fact, that men were sitting there. When O'Higgins left Dunamase to go to church he did not bother to call his personal guard, who had accompanied him on the swimming excursion earlier in the morning. His wife was in the hall arranging flowers; he kissed her, and went to see his daughter, Maeve, who was playing with her toys. The child had first to be kissed, then the dolls in turn, and finally Una, the baby of the family, asleep in her pram. A policeman stood on duty at the side gate of the garden through which O'Higgins passed. A few minutes later a burst of revolver fire was heard coming from the road. Hogan [Patrick Hogan, O'Higgins' best pal, and Minister for Agriculture, who was visiting the O'Higginses], who was waiting for a friend to take him out to play golf, ran from the house, revolver in hand, in the direction of the shooting.
>
> Dunamase is only a few hundred yards from the corner where Booterstown Avenue joins Cross Avenue, and, as O'Higgins approached the turn in the road, a boy on a bicycle gave a signal to a motor-car which was parked on the side of the road. A man came out and fired at point-blank range. O'Higgins turned and tried to run for cover to the gate of Sans Souci, a house on the other side of the road. His attacker followed, firing as he ran;

O'Higgins had only strength to cross the road. On the other side he fell upon the path, whereupon two other men rushed out from behind the car and fired at him as he lay upon the ground. One stood across the body, pouring the contents of his revolver into it. [Harling claimed that the police suspected that the two men sitting on the seat were assigned to take out the bodyguard.] The murder party then drove away, and the first person to arrive on the scene was an old colleague, Eoin MacNeill.

O'Higgins was alive, but in dreadful agony. One bullet had entered the head behind the ear. Six were in his body. But he had not lost consciousness, and when MacNeill bent over him, he murmured: 'I forgive my murderers,' and then, after a pause while he collected strength to speak, he said: 'Tell my wife I love her eternally.' The discipline with which he had habitually controlled his mind did not leave him now, and lying weltering in his blood on the dusty road in the torrid midday sun, he dictated a will. A priest came and administered the Last Sacraments, a doctor was summoned and attended him there on the side of the road until an ambulance arrived.

'I couldn't help it,' he said to his wife when they carried him into his house and laid him on an improvised bed on the dining-room floor. 'I did my best.'

He lay pale but fully conscious, speaking slowly and clearly. That he was going to die he was quite certain, but he was gay in the face of death. Of himself, or his pain, he never spoke, but he asked for each of his family in turn and sent messages to those who were away. Again and again he affirmed that he forgave his murderers. To his wife he said: 'You must have no bitterness in your heart for them.' Then remembering the problem with which the Government would be faced, he exclaimed: 'My colleagues! My poor colleagues!' His friend, Surgeon Barniville, who had been summoned from a distance, arrived early, and noticing his pain, lay down to support him with his arm. 'Barney hasn't had his lunch,' said O'Higgins, looking up at his wife: to each of those who tended him he had a word of thanks and apology for the trouble he was giving. A doctor offered brandy. He refused it. 'Every man ought to drink his quota,' he said; 'I have drunk mine in my day.' Of de Valera, he said: 'Tell my colleagues that they must beware of him in public life; he will play down to the weaknesses of the people.'

He spoke of death. His wife said: 'You will be with your father and Michael Collins and your little son.' He smiled and pictured himself sitting on a damp cloud with a harp, arguing about politics with Mick.

'Do you mind dying, Kevin?' his wife asked. A smile came over his face and he replied, 'Mind dying? Why should I? My hour has come. My job is done.' When his friend, Patrick Hogan, knelt beside him, he said: 'I loved you, Hogan. Good-bye, boss. We never had a row.'

Hogan whispered: 'You can die happy, Kevin.'

O'Higgins lived for five hours in terrible pain.

He was thirty-five years old when he was gunned down. It was later reported that some eye-witnesses claimed to have heard O'Higgins saying, as he looked up at his killers, 'I know who you are and I know why you are doing this but let this be the last of the killing.'

The assassination of the minister for justice stunned the populace, but no one was more shocked than Éamon de Valera, who was electioneering in Ennis, County Clare when he heard the news. It seems that he went into a fit of rage, for he must have realised that those who had killed Kevin O'Higgins had also killed his chances of becoming president of the next Free State government.

De Valera moved quickly to distance himself and Fianna Fáil from the brutal killing. On Monday, 11 July he issued the following statement to the press:

The assassination of Mr O'Higgins is murder, and is inexcusable from any standpoint. I am confident that no republican organisation was responsible for it or would give it any countenance. It is the duty of every citizen to set his face against anything of this kind. It is a crime that cuts at the root of representative government, and no one who realises what the crime means can do otherwise than deplore and condemn it. Every right-minded individual will deeply sympathise with the bereaved widow in her agony.

De Valera was not betraying his naivety when he said that 'no republican organisation ... would give it any countenance'. Rather, he was expressing a heartfelt disgust and anger at the assassination and was reassuring the Irish people that he was totally against using any type of violence to further his cause. Let us not forget, however, that Kevin O'Higgins was a figure of intense hatred for republicans then and indeed is for some of them to this very day. De Valera's speech of five years earlier, where he talked of 'wading through Irish blood', must surely have come home to haunt him that day.

Seán Harling reported that 'four years after the civil war had ended, the Specials were told by their spies in the IRA of the existence of a hard core of about twenty dedicated Dublin IRA volunteers who had liberty of action. They knew who at least six of them were and believed that O'Higgins' killers came from that group. But they had no way of proving it.' Harling also said that 'those in Fianna Fáil who knew who was responsible for the assassination of Kevin O'Higgins kept de Valera in the dark about it all those years'. And he added, 'I don't know whether Frank Aiken knew who had carried out the assassination but I do know that it was he more than anyone else who wanted me shot dead.'

Cosgrave's government was devastated by the killing and dreaded more attacks on cabinet members. They even feared a police backlash. They were in total disarray for some time, but when they pulled themselves together they used O'Higgins' killing to introduce further repressive legislation. Harling said, 'O'Higgins might have forgiven his killers, but his colleagues in government, particularly the Specials, did not. They were gunning for revenge.'

The government introduced three bills. The first was the Public Safety Bill, which gave them the power to arrest people they suspected of being members or supporters of an illegal organisation. They could pull them off the streets or drag them out of their beds without a warrant, then haul them before a military court or simply intern them without trial. Secondly, they pulled the rug from under de Valera's feet by abolishing Article 48, the referendum clause in the constitution, which de Valera was in the process of using to avoid taking the oath.

The third piece of legislation was the Electoral Amendment Bill – the stunner. It was designed, one might believe, to put de Valera on the hot seat. It required every candidate in every election to sign an affidavit that he or she would take both his or her seat and the oath of allegiance to the British crown if elected, or else be disqualified. Fianna Fáil, therefore, must either accept the democratic legitimacy of Dáil Éireann and take their seats, or give up politics forever.

The Specials used the first bill to great effect. They carried out raids on the homes of known IRA members and republican sympathisers throughout Dublin city and county in an all-out effort to capture O'Higgins' killers. They brought in dozens for questioning, ten of whom were high-ranking officers in the Dublin Brigade (ex-Fianna scout Joseph Reynolds was one of them). They were charged with conspiring to kill O'Higgins but were released without charge after three weeks in custody.

The Specials gleaned the names of four or five likely suspects from a couple of prisoners during their always heavy-handed and sometimes brutal interrogations in secluded police cells. The arresting officers were Superintendent Ennis, Inspector Kinsella and Detective Sergeants Hughes, Mooney and Byrne – all colleagues of Harling's.

According to Seán Harling, the Specials were reasonably satisfied from information received that they could at least guess who two of the assassins might be, but they knew it would be a complete waste of time to bring them in for questioning. 'They had to let them off the hook for now and bide their time,' said Harling. Seán Harling also reported, 'General O'Duffy went looking for permission from his government colleagues to have his men gun down all the known IRA members of the Dublin Brigade.'

It was now Fianna Fáil's turn to be thrown into disarray. They would be disqualified from entering another election unless they signed the affidavit stating that they would take the hated oath. They were left with only two options – either walk away from politics altogether or take the oath of allegiance to the British crown. One of them, Patrick Belton, put his political career first after reading the legislation and took the oath. De Valera claimed, 'Belton, since his election, had been manoeuvring for an opportunity to go in and take the oath.' He was instantly expelled from Fianna Fáil for 'going wrong'. Dan Breen, seeing the futility of being outside the Dáil, it was said, became the first anti-Treaty republican to take his seat as an independent republican.

But de Valera, it seems, was determined to enter Leinster House and to bring the other forty-two elected Fianna Fáil deputies with him. On 9 August, he called a meeting of the Fianna Fáil executive to debate the consequences of not taking their seats. It seems that he told them he believed that they should take their seats or give up political agitation altogether, for he saw no alternative. They passed a resolution permitting their elected deputies to decide whether they wanted to enter the Free State Dáil. The republican ethos and the principles over which the first split and the terrible civil war took place were about to be put to the test.

The forty-three deputies met the next evening and decided unanimously to enter Leinster House. De Valera presented a statement, which was signed by all Fianna Fáil deputies, to the press the next morning. They were about to let the country know that they were going in and, according to republican ethos, 'going wrong'.

On 11 August 1927, de Valera arrived once again at the gates of Leinster House, telling Colm Ó Murchadha that he was there this time to sign the declaration. Frank Aiken, his chief of staff, and Dr James Ryan stood beside him, bearing witness to what he was about to do and say. De Valera read out a speech in Irish, which Ó Murchadha told him he wasn't interested in. All he wanted was de Valera's signature in the book, representing allegiance to the British crown.

It was later said by de Valera's detractors that he had taken the ostrich approach to the signing of the declaration, because with pen in hand he had said to Colm Ó Murchadha, 'I am not prepared to take an oath. I am prepared to put my name down in this book in order to get permission to go into the Dáil.'

He then brushed the bible aside, covered the wording of the declaration with some papers, and signed it blindly, saying to Ó Murchadha, 'You must remember I am taking no oath.'

'Well, if dat's not buryin' yer head in the sand, I don' know what is', an old Dubliner was heard to remark when he was told.

De Valera left the building in a huff, saying that one day he would burn that bloody book with his signature in it.

Fianna Fáil's decision to take their seats and to sign the oath of allegiance to the British crown was, it seems, taken by most as de Valera and the vast majority of the republican family finally accepting partition and the Free State Dáil as the legitimate seat of the nation's government. Sinn Féin, however, interpreted it as the final betrayal:

Oh he's gone an' done the villain,
An' took the dirty shillin'.
Hope he chokes to death,
While swillin' in the mornin'.

When the forty-three Fianna Fáil deputies entered Dáil Éireann on 12 August they were all – except de Valera, according to reports – carrying arms, expecting a gunfight to erupt in the chamber. They joined with Labour in demanding that the Electoral Amendment Bill be suspended pending a referendum. Their demand failed and the bill was passed into law.

But they were not defeated yet. Tom Johnson (leader of the Labour party) and Captain John Redmond (leader of the National League) agreed to form a coalition government, which would be supported by Fianna Fáil, and even had the gall to try and woo the five Sinn Féin deputies into taking their seats and entering into the pact. But Austin Stack's Sinn Féin would not hear of it.

On 16 August Tom Johnson moved a vote of no confidence in the government. The vote ended in a tie because Vincent Rice, a member of the National League, voted against it and another of Redmond's party, Alderman John Jinks, did not turn up. The chairman cast his deciding vote in favour of the government. De Valera, it appeared, was jinxed.

Then, shortly after the government had won the vote, they dropped a bombshell that shattered the aspirations of all the other parties, except Fianna Fáil. Cosgrave's party had won two pending by-elections and Cosgrave believed, wrongly as it turned out, that the people wanted him back in control. He dissolved the government and called a snap general election. De Valera called it sharp practice, but the Fianna Fáil party was ready for the fight.

The election was held on 15 September and Fianna Fáil won fifty-seven seats. Sinn Féin could not contest the election. Redmond's National League was decimated and Tom Johnson lost his seat.

The state of the parties after the election was as follows:

Cumann na nGaedheal:	62
Fianna Fáil:	57
Labour:	13
Independents:	12
Farmers' party:	6
National League:	2
Independent Labour:	1

De Valera was certain that, with the support of the Labour party and some sympathetic independents, he would head the government of the fifth Dáil. He had changed his mind once again and was now actively seeking the support of other parties to gain the power his detractors said he so coveted. However, it was Cosgrave who, with the support of the Farmers' party, the National League and most independents, became taoiseach of the fifth Dáil.

When Countess Markievicz died on 15 July 1927, the Fianna general headquarters selected Harling to take charge of her funeral procession. They were soon to be in for a further revelation about him.

Harling called a meeting on Saturday, 16 July to finalise the arrangements for the procession. Several prominent Fianna members attended, including John Murray, Thomas Mullins and Barney Mellows. Harling suggested to them that they should form a new militant organisation. Mellows smelled a rat and proposed that they should wait a couple of weeks after the countess' funeral before discussing his suggestion. He was suspicious as to why Harling wanted to return to militancy. He advised Murray, Mullins and the others to give him a wide berth, but Murray was curious to know what Harling was up to and arranged to meet him a week after the funeral.

When Murray and some others met Harling a week later he suggested that they should form a new and independent republican army called the Clann Breasna. Murray asked where they were going to get the arms for this new army. Harling said they would have to carry out raids, but that would come later. First they would need a typewriter. Murray pointed out that they did not have the funds to buy a typewriter, but Harling suggested that he knew where they could steal one: the Fianna Éireann offices in Drury Street. A couple of nights later Harling and a few others burgled the Fianna office and stole the typewriter.

At a meeting the day after the burglary, Harling revealed his master plan for the procurement of weapons for their new army. The Baden Powell scouting organisation still underwent military training at special weekend and annual training camps. Harling of course knew the halls where the military equipment was stored. The Clann Breasna, led by him, would raid these halls and seize the weapons. The volunteers would then have to find safe houses or secret dugouts to dump the arms.

The Specials would have had a field day uncovering those dumps and arresting their caretakers. But they were deprived of that pleasure, because nobody joined Harling's organisation. Clann Breasna died before it was ever born.

Harling had become over-confident and careless. He was making it glaringly obvious to those that believed he had 'gone wrong' that his role as a mere spy had changed to that of *agent provocateur*. The cat was out of the bag at last. He resigned from the Fianna. His companions who had vigorously defended his honour were devastated. He had betrayed their faith and trust in him. Where once in their hearts they held nothing but respect, love and admiration for Seán Harling, they now harboured deep hatred, bitterness and a lust for revenge.

By the end of July the Specials had reported to the government that they suspected the killers of their minister for justice, Kevin O'Higgins, were members of both Fianna Fáil and the IRA. The government was running scared, thinking that more among them had been singled out for assassination. They were at pains to know if the killing had been organised by certain members of Fianna Fáil, or if it had indeed been an opportunist murder by volunteers with liberty of action. According to Harling, there were well-placed members of Fianna Fáil who wanted to know that as well.

The government instructed the Specials to acquire a copy of Fianna Fáil's real constitution. They were anxious to know whether it endorsed the carrying and use of arms by certain of its members – and if it did, did they have liberty of action?

David Neligan, who received the order directly from Eoin O'Duffy, instructed Harling to join Fianna Fáil. His mission was to gain the confidence of known militants of that organisation and try and glean who had killed O'Higgins and what their real policy was on weapons. He was also to obtain a copy of their real constitution. Harling was reluctant to comply with this instruction but Broy and another person reassured him that he would meet with no hassle when he applied for a job with Fianna Fáil.

They were right. Harling encountered no problem in obtaining a position of employment in Fianna Fáil, despite the very dark cloud of suspicion hanging over him. Someone in Fianna Fáil must have vouched for him. Perhaps it was one of those members who were also anxious to know if the assassins of Kevin O'Higgins were members of their organisation.

Harling's membership of Fianna Fáil was short lived. He was unmasked by three of his old Fianna Éireann comrades, Murray, Mullins and Mellows, who vengefully presented evidence of the recent shenanigans in Fianna Éireann to a couple of Fianna Fáil senior officers. Harling headed for the door post-haste. Indeed, he was practically chased out by Frank Aiken.

But how much information received by the Specials could the republicans really lay at Harling's door? They had no concrete evidence against him. They could point to no specific case where a volunteer actually went to prison, save for the Healy affair, or where volunteers' homes had been raided and dumps uncovered because of Harling. However, the Specials had uncovered a sizeable and newly established IRA arms dump on the north side of Dublin city. The republicans did not really know who had given it away but they credited Harling with it. Encouraged by Seán Russell and Frank Aiken – who a week after Countess Markievicz's funeral had asked Harling to attend an IRA court martial (Harling had told them to go and get lost with themselves) – and considering Harling's recent episode in the Fianna, the republican movement now fully accepted Healy's account of the affair that put him in prison as true.

Even though Fianna Fáil had accepted the democratic legitimacy of the Free State Dáil, they still had not decommissioned their weapons and were still drilling their secret army. It was two volunteers from that secret army who were sent out to Woodpark lodge on that cold January evening in 1928 to kill Special Intelligence Officer Seán Harling.

Chapter 8

From Heroes to Rogues

The Redican brothers emerged from prison bitter men, especially James, who believed that some unidentified IRA officers were to blame for their continued incarceration. He was told that all his old bank-raiding comrades from the South Westmeath Brigade had sided with the Irregulars in the civil war, and that they all joined Fianna Fáil when it was formed in 1926. Redican had no time for Fianna Fáil and always referred to them as 'that lot' when they were mentioned in his company. Some of the IRA officers in Dublin whom he had derided for not turning out in 1916 were now high-ranking Fianna Fáilers, and he suspected that they were the cause of his being sent back to prison in March 1922.

The brothers dutifully reported once a week to their local garda station at first. But after five months they got itchy feet and were gunning for action – in particular, for revenge for what they believed was their illegal incarceration.

In December 1924 James wrote to the Department of Justice asking the minister to relieve them from the obligation of reporting to the police, as they intended to emigrate. The minister remitted the obligation but they would remain ticket-of-leave men.

The brothers didn't emigrate, however. Instead, they went to Sligo town, where James set himself up in his old profession, as a bookmaker. When the local gardaí found out he was in town, they placed him under surveillance. But he left Sligo town in a hurry, owing money to some punters who had laid bets with him (the local gardaí reported to Dublin that he was a 'welshing bookie'), and went to Castlebaldwin, Riverstown, County Sligo.

Thomas stayed on in Sligo town, where he took part in a couple of sorties with the local IRA. He got fed up after only six weeks, however, and returned to Dublin, to the Redicans' new address at Woodpark lodge on the Dartry Road. Thomas was a motor driver by trade and got temporary work for a number of companies for very low pay. He befriended the Countess Markievicz and became one of her chauffeurs from late 1925 until she was admitted to hospital in July 1927. He said that the countess called her car 'Tin Lizzie'.

Times were hard and getting harder and finding employment with a living wage – indeed any sort of employment – was almost impossible for an ex-prisoner like Thomas Redican. He made up his mind that if he could not find a decent job soon he would have to emigrate or, 'to earn a few bob', he would join the Free State army.

Meanwhile, in Castlebaldwin, James Redican was being kept under surveillance by the local gardaí, who reported to Dublin:

> James Joseph Redican, since his arrival in Castlebaldwin, has been associating with prominent Irregulars – amongst them being his landlord Bart Chambers and Roger Brennan, two of the best known republicans in the area. He spends his time spreading sedition and preaching against the government – principally in public houses. He is suspected of organising for the Irish republican army. The gardaí, however, are unable to bring any substantial charge against him but keep him under a strict supervision.

James Redican was now a maverick, one of that breed of men who cannot abide rules and regulations and who will not accept discipline. But he was a republican and very useful to the IRA, who used his services whenever he made himself available to them, even though he was incapacitated by his near-crippling war wounds.

On 15 August 1926, Superintendent D. O'Shea of Riverstown received information that James Redican and Bart Chambers were about to carry out a clandestine operation on behalf of the local IRA. The next day, he dispatched Sergeant Healy and a couple of other officers to intercept the two men. Sergeant Healy arrested them and brought them to Riverstown barracks, where he wrote in his report:

> I found Redican hiding in a cartload of sheep, in a cart driven by Bart Chambers. Redican was completely hidden in the cart and would not have been seen by us were it not for the information we had received. Redican gave me a wrong name when I arrested him; the name he gave was – Keilty – his mother's maiden name. But when I cautioned him about lying and told him we knew who he was, he stated he was better known as James Redican. Bart Chambers denied knowing Redican was in the cart and we had to release him.

Superintendent O'Shea charged Redican with having broken two of the conditions of his licence, namely 'that he was found in such circumstances as would lead the gardaí and the court to suspect that he was about to commit a felony' and 'being unable while in custody to produce his licence when asked for it by a guard'. He was brought before Riverstown District Court on 28 August. Bail was allowed but was not forthcoming. He was convicted, sentenced to six weeks' imprisonment and further bound to be of good behaviour and to keep the peace for three months. He later secured the necessary bail and was released from custody.

James Redican returned to Dublin but could not find employment. He was of course near-unemployable because of his wounds, but his slim chances of getting a job were not augmented by his reputation. He tried all sorts of scams to earn a living, including setting himself up as a 'private inquiry agency' under his old pseudonym, Thomas Casey, at his old bookmaker's address in Bray.

One particular case in 1927 put an end to his private inquiry business. He was hired by a Mrs Goddard to go to a house in Sandycove and collect some furniture and other chattels she had left there for safekeeping. When he pressed her, however, she confessed that she and a friend, a Mr Leahy, had left the items there in lieu of rent they owed.

On 4 April James Redican knocked on the door of 11 Summerhill Road, Sandycove, and introduced himself to the owner, Mrs Daft, as a member of the Detective Branch from Pearse Street garda station. He said he had been sent there by his superior, Sergeant Cullinan, to collect some items of furniture left there by a man named Leahy in lieu of rent he owed. Leahy, he said, was in custody back in Pearse Street and the furniture was now required in court for identification purposes. Mrs Daft believed his story and handed over the furniture.

A month later Mr and Mrs Daft turned up at Pearse Street station enquiring about the outcome of the Leahy case and the whereabouts of the furniture. Sergeant Cullinan blew a fuse when he heard their story. When he heard the description of the impersonator, however, he knew whom he would be looking for. The police recovered the furniture from a garage in Rathmines where Redican had stored it. He was brought before Justice Collins, found guilty of impersonating a police officer and fined five pounds. The money was immediately paid into court and he was released. After that episode the order of obligation providing that Redican report weekly to his local garda station was reimposed.

Later that year the body of an alleged informer, a man called Fox, was found in Orwell Park with gunshot wounds to the head. James Redican became a suspect and was promptly arrested and brought to Rathmines garda station for interrogation. He was released without charge.

When Redican chanced his arm again, asking to be released from the obligation of reporting to the police, the Ministry of Home Affairs and the Department of Justice expressed serious concern about his recent activities. They had received complaints about his conduct over the past year, some of which concerned his association with other men's wives and the use of threats towards others. Also, the Prisons Board informed the gardaí that they 'regarded Redican as a most clever and dangerous man. He has a very long remnant [nearly 12 years] and we are willing to give him one last chance but he should be severely cautioned as to the consequences of any further breach of the law on his part.' They ordered that his obligation of reporting to the police once a week should not be remitted.

When Harling arrived for work at Pearse Street garda station one evening in late August 1927 he was told by the desk sergeant to report urgently to Superintendent O'Driscoll's office. When he entered the office he was startled to find Broy, Mulcahy, Neligan, O'Driscoll, O'Duffy and Henry O'Friel of the Department of Justice there, each with a worried expression across his brow. O'Driscoll told him that they had received very reliable intelligence that a death sentence had been passed upon him by the IRA.

Harling was stunned and upset but not surprised at the news. He had half expected it and it occurred to him that if he had not refused to attend their court martial three weeks earlier his corpse would be rotting into the soil by now. O'Duffy advised him to move from his house on the Rathmines Road to a safer abode as soon as possible.

That evening, while travelling home on the tram meditating on his predicament, Harling suddenly and involuntarily exclaimed aloud, 'Jesus, that bollix Aiken! That fucking bollix Aiken!' The other two passengers gaped at him, obviously thinking he must have a screw loose.

He decided not to tell his wife the bad news because he did not want to upset her, but he spent a restless night considering what to do. He definitely did not want to uproot his wife and baby daughter from their cosy apartment, knowing where they would have to go if he did. He thought it best to take a chance and stay, hoping that things might just blow over.

But it soon became apparent that things were not going to blow over. The very next morning when he pulled the bedroom blinds he noticed a couple of dodgy-looking characters across the road wearing trenchcoats and soft hats. They seemed to be watching the house and they followed him to and from work that day and the next. He had no choice now but to tell his wife and move out quickly.

When Henry O'Friel was informed about the men watching Harling, he ordered that Harling be immediately issued with a revolver for self-protection.

Harling explained his predicament to his mother-in-law and asked her if they could stay at Woodpark lodge for a short time. She agreed, without consulting with her family, that they could move in, but only when they could do it unbeknown to the IRA watchers.

Although he did not relish the thought of subjecting his wife and child to the constraints of that little gate lodge after their previous experience there, Harling was convinced that they would be much safer there than anywhere else. The IRA, he reasoned, would not dare attack the Redican home for fear of a reprisal attack by James and Thomas Redican – two of the most feared and respected men in the city, even by the police. They had access to weapons and would not hesitate to use them against anyone who would dare attack their family and home. The IRA high command were aware of this.

At twelve noon on the last Saturday of August 1927, the men watching Harling's apartment on the Rathmines Road were picked up by the Specials and taken away for questioning. This of course was a ruse, prearranged to give Harling, who was watching the proceedings from his bedroom window, the chance to slip out of the house with his wife and child and retreat to Woodpark lodge.

As Harling and Nora approached the door of the two-bed-roomed gate lodge, they could hear the excited chatter. Inside were the father, the mother and their sons James, Thomas, Patrick and Laurence. The cause of the excitement was that Thomas had just joined the Free State army. He had decided not to emigrate, but had waited until a couple of weeks had elapsed after the Countess Markievicz's funeral before joining up. He was leaving that afternoon for the Curragh training camp in County Kildare.

'Where do you think you're bloody well going?' Thomas barked when Harling appeared at the door with his wife and child, dragging their belongings behind them.

'They're moving in, Tom,' the mother told him.

'They're fucking well what?' exclaimed Thomas, who had a most foul tongue. 'I haven't set foot outside the door yet and he's moving in? Did he lose his job in Barden's garage or what?'

'No, it's nothing like that, Tom,' the mother answered. 'Look, sit down all of you,' she ordered. 'Come on Tom, sit down. Seán has something to tell us. And it's just as well you hadn't left for the Curragh yet for its best that all of you hear this together.'

They had an idea what was coming, for they too had heard the rumours going around town about their brother-in-law and had defended his honour, with fisticuffs, in public houses.

Harling confirmed to his dumbfounded in-laws that he had joined the Free State secret service and that his job in Barden's garage was only a cover. The Redican siblings somehow managed to hold their composure when they heard this devastating but not unexpected news – except Thomas, of course.

'Why you little bollix, you!' was his initial reply. James' reaction was more considered.

'Well, that's the rumours we've heard about you confirmed now, Seán.'

'Why did you do it, Seán?' asked a worried Laurence.

'For certain considerations, Laurence,' was his short reply.

'And I don't suppose that those certain considerations included thirty pieces of silver, Seán?' Thomas cynically asked. Harling ignored him.

The mother had not uttered a word. She sat there in knowledgeable silence. James, who had being eyeing her with suspicion, said, 'You knew about this right from the start, Mother, didn't you?'

'I did, James,' she replied, guiltily. 'Dorothy told me.'

'When did she tell you, mother?' asked James.

'A couple of days before the baby was born,' she replied, looking at Thomas as she answered.

'But that was a year ago!' exploded Thomas.

'I know, I know,' replied the mother, showing some agitation.

'And you, father?' asked James.

'No, James,' interjected the mother, answering for him. 'Your father didn't know anything about it until just now, like the rest of you.'

'If you'd have told us sooner, Mother, Tom and I wouldn't have gotten into the scraps we did with some republicans, defending Seán's honour when all the time the whispers about him were true,' James told her.

'And why didn't you tell us, Mother?' asked Laurence.

'Because Dorothy pleaded with me not to tell any of you until she and Seán thought the time was right,' answered the mother.

James turned to Harling, 'And the time is right now, Seán, is it?'

'Yes,' replied Harling. 'It is, James.'

'And why now, Seán?' enquired James.

'Because they now know for definite,' replied Harling with a nonchalant shrug of the shoulders. He did not mention that he had a Fianna Fáil/IRA death sentence hanging over him, but the brothers guessed as much. Why else would he be seeking sanctuary at Woodpark lodge?

'So they're on to you, Seán. And you think you'll be safer here than at your own place?' James asked him.

'Yes, James, I do,' Harling replied confidently. 'It will be much safer here, especially for Nora and the baby.'

'Yes, it will, Seán, but did you give a curse about the trouble that will surely be visited on this house and family because of what you have done?' Thomas interjected angrily.

'What are you talking about?' retorted Harling. 'Aren't you joining the Free State army?'

'Yes, I am,' replied Thomas. 'But I'm not joining to spy for them. It will be just a week's wages to me.'

The Redicans, now fully aware of Harling's impending fate and the danger posed to them if they allowed him to live in their home, were faced with a terrible dilemma. They could not very well toss their only sister and baby niece out onto the street with him, but they did not want him to stay.

So James, speaking for the others, said, 'Seán, Nora, if you're going to live here with us I want both of you to understand very clearly that our priority, that is Tom and me, is to defend our family and home from attack. Seán, you'll have to take your chances when you're abroad.' Then he remarked, 'I suppose we'll all have to be looking over our shoulders from now on.'

'God help us all,' said the father softly, rising from the table and shuffling off into his bedroom.

'God can't help us now, Father!' Thomas shouted after him.

The house lapsed into silence for a moment, then James asked Harling, 'What were you thinking of, Seán, turning your coat just like that? I mean you being so close to de Valera and all?'

'I didn't just turn my coat, James,' replied Harling. 'As you know, they had been working on me for months to get me to change, roughing me up first, then soft soaping me with yarns about Dev going to break from Sinn Féin and us all being one again. They told me if I joined them and spied on the Fianna I would help smooth Dev's path to Leinster House.'

'And you swallowed that load of bollocks hook, line and sinker. You eejit,' interjected Thomas.

'No, I didn't swallow anything, Tom,' retorted Harling, disgusted that he could be thought an eejit by the likes of Thomas Redican. 'I didn't believe them. I knew they were just buttering me up. They obviously believed I was still close to Dev.'

'And aren't you, Seán?' asked James.

'Not really, James,' replied Harling, and hurriedly went on. 'At the beginning of June last year Nora and I were really on our uppers. We had little or no food on the table, as you all were well aware, and the baby on the way and all. My back was to the wall. Besides, I was getting increasingly disillusioned with our own lot, and apart from you none of them offered us the slightest bit of help. So after prolonged discussions with Nora, and with her encouragement and blessing, I joined them. And that's it.'

'And did anyone else, other than the Staters, encourage you to change, Seán?' asked James, suspiciously.

'No,' replied Harling sharply.

'So your decision to turn was a purely bread-and-butter one?' suggested James.

'Jesus Seán!' yelped Patrick. 'I'd rather beg for a living.'

Ignoring Patrick, Harling answered James's question.

'Not entirely, James, for when de Valera did split from Sinn Féin I thought, my Jaysus, the so-and-sos were right after all. And the thoughts of what Mulcahy had told me about Dev winning the next election and how we would all be working for him were running through my mind. I thought, well, if Dev is doing it one way, why can't I do it another way?' Then he added, strangely, 'We know that Dev is fearful of another O'Higgins-type atrocity happening. Something like that could ruin his chances of ever becoming taoiseach.'

James questioned Harling about what he meant by Dev doing it one way and him doing it another, but he refused to elaborate. (In fact, though David Neligan was of the opinion that 'it was poverty drove him to join us', that was the only reason Harling ever gave to anyone for turning his coat.)

James then turned to his sister and bluntly said, 'Nora, you must surely know that when they catch up with Seán, he will be a dead man.' Nora burst into tears and was comforted by her worried mother.

Thomas stood up and said, 'Well, I better get going if I'm to catch my train. I've heard enough of this shite anyway. Goodbye everyone, see you on my first home leave. Mother, say goodbye to Father for me, will you?'

As he made for the door, James shouted, 'Hold up there, Tom! I'll walk you to the tram.'

James wanted to discuss tactics with him in case the house should be attacked. Both agreed that it would not be long before the IRA found out where Harling was living. They would put him and the house under surveillance and make the attempt to kill him when the opportunity presented itself. The brothers agreed that if Harling was attacked on his way to or from work, so be it. But if the IRA attacked their home to get him they would defend it vigorously.

'Good luck to you, Tom, and take care of yourself down there,' said James.

'I'll see you so, Jim,' replied Thomas. 'And keep your ear to the ground. Goodbye for now, and may God bless you all.'

James's two younger siblings were engaged in a shouting match with Harling when he returned to the lodge. They were cursing him for what he had done. Because of him the IRA would surely attack the house and kill them all. Harling was telling them that he had done it to put bread and butter on the table for their sister and baby niece.

'Stop it!' yelled James. 'We're in trouble enough without you shouting and bawling at one another. You'd be better employed directing your energy to praying and hoping that the IRA leave us and our home out of it.'

'There's nothing to worry about anyway, lads. We'll be safe enough here,' said Harling reassuringly. 'There'll be armed members of the Detective Branch keeping watch on the house, and I'll be armed at all times.'

'Is that so, Seán?' said James, cynically. 'Don't forget, they got to Kevin O'Higgins, the minister for justice, and I'm certain they'll get to you too if they have a mind to.'

Upon hearing this, Harling's wife broke down again and was once more comforted by her mother.

Chapter 9

The Attack

It was not long before Fianna Fáil and the IRA found out where Harling was living and put the house under surveillance. And it was not long either before the Redicans noticed that their home was being watched by men dressed in those featureless long trenchcoats and soft hats, sitting on the seat opposite the lodge. Sometimes, too, a car with four men in it would drive slowly up and down the road, slowing down even more as they passed the lodge. They noticed that the men in the trenchcoats would move off when they saw the car approaching.

The mother, sister, Patrick and Laurence attached no significance to this, thinking it was just the police changing shifts. Patrick and Laurence, believing that the men in the trenchcoats were gardaí, gave them a friendly wave when leaving or entering the lodge. These gestures of friendliness infuriated the watchers, who thought the two lads were making fun them. But with memories of the nights when their home had been raided by the Black and Tans looking for James and Thomas – especially that cold December night when their mother had been pistol whipped – they were afraid of visits from the IRA, and felt somewhat secure in the idea that they were being protected by the now-friendly police.

But James knew that the watchers in trenchcoats were IRA volunteers gathering intelligence on Harling's movements, who would move off when they saw either him or the car, which did contain detectives, approaching.

Harling did not go out much at night or on his days off and he never varied his routine. He left the house at the same time every day to go to his place of work, Pearse Street garda station, and returned at the same time every evening. This made his movements easy to log for his watchers, who were also staking out the police station, though much less often and much less obviously than Harling's home.

When Thomas Redican arrived home on Christmas leave in 1927, his brother James was the only one at home. He was babysitting his niece. Patrick and Laurence were at work; the father was out tending the gardens of Woodpark; Harling was out doing his secret-service work; and the mother and sister were Christmas shopping. Thomas walked through the door and went straight to the tiny kitchen window. He looked out, then turned and asked his brother, 'How long have those two fuckers across the road been watching the house, Jim?'

'Oh, about three and a half months now,' replied James, adding sarcastically, 'And hello to you too, Tom.'

'Oh, I'm sorry, Jim, hello,' replied Thomas, taking his brother's hand and shaking it firmly and warmly. He turned back to look out the window again, saying, 'And who are they?'

'They're the IRA, Tom,' answered James solemnly.

After a lull, James asked, 'How are you getting on in the army, Tom?'

'Oh just fine, Jim,' replied a clearly agitated Thomas. 'Is it always the same two doing the watching?'

'No, Tom, they vary the men and times.'

'And do you know or recognise any of them at all, Jim?' asked Thomas.

'Sometimes, maybe,' James answered, shrugging his shoulders.

'And those two out there now, Jim, do you recognise them?'

'I'm not certain, but I think they're young Coughlan and Doyle,' replied James, glancing out the window.

'Jaysus Christ!' exclaimed Thomas.

'Sounds like you've heard of them,' remarked James.

'Who in our circles hasn't, Jim?' answered Thomas, adding, 'And they're the last two people in the world a man would want coming after him.'

Then, in afterthought, Thomas asked, 'Would you say they're armed?'

'It's highly unlikely, Tom, because a few of them were pulled in by the Specials for loitering. When they were searched they were found to be unarmed.' The brothers knew that it was a standard order in the IRA never to be armed while gathering intelligence on someone.

'Do you think we should go out and warn them about attacking the house?' asked a now-gung-ho Thomas.

'No, I think we should leave well enough alone for the time being. Besides, I've been assured by my contacts in the IRA that our house is not a target and will not be attacked.'

'Do you think it's likely to be those two?' asked Thomas.

'More than likely, Tom, more than likely,' answered his brother, meditatively looking out the window at the two men.

James was jolted out of his reverie by the sudden and noisy entrance of his mother and sister home from town. The mother was bellowing from the hallway, 'I see the police are keeping a watchful eye on the house again, James!' James and Thomas stared at each other, making no comment. Then the mother, noticing Thomas as she entered the kitchen, let out a shriek of delight and threw her arms lovingly around him. Amid all the excitement, tears, hugs and kisses, the two men outside, for the moment, were forgotten.

Despite their fear and apprehension, the Redicans enjoyed a relaxed, peaceful and undisturbed Christmas that year. And on the day after St Stephen's day, Thomas bid them goodbye and headed back to the Curragh.

The surveillance of the Redican home by Fianna Fáil/IRA volunteers continued throughout the month of January 1928, although on a much less frequent basis than during the previous three and a half months. The Redicans, then, were able to enjoy a relatively relaxed start to the new year.

Thomas Redican arrived home at 3 p.m. on Saturday, 28 January 1928 on a surprise three-days' leave from the Curragh and brought to the house a short period of great joviality. Amid the excitement of his homecoming he expressed surprise at the absence of surveillance on the house. The mother worriedly told him, 'The police for some reason have eased up a bit on their watching of us since the beginning of the new year.'

'That's a good sign, surely,' replied Thomas, trying to ease his mother's concern.

'Wishful thinking, Tom,' interjected James. He beckoned Tom aside and said that Superintendent O'Driscoll had told Seán that the easing off of the surveillance was just the calm before the storm.

At about half past six that evening, while the Redicans were quietly relaxing, there came a sudden and violent outburst of gunfire close to the lodge. Bullets seemed to be bouncing off the walls and the roof of the house. Pandemonium and panic erupted in their little home and all dived for cover under the small kitchen table – except Nora, who snatched her little daughter from the floor and covered her with her own body in a corner to shield her from any stray bullets that might enter the kitchen.

James was furious with the IRA, but he only added to the panic and fear when he started shouting repeatedly, 'The bastards told me they wouldn't attack the house! The bastards!'

All went silent for a couple of minutes, then two more shots rang out in quick succession. They heard running footsteps and the front door slamming, then Harling's voice shouting, 'The house is under attack!' When Harling suddenly appeared at the kitchen door, gun in hand, James flung a bucket of water at him, the only weapon he could lay his hands on, thinking he was one of the attackers. When they realised he was not being pursued into the house, Thomas ran and bolted the door. The father ran for his bedroom to seek sanctuary.

Outside, a man wearing a long black coat was seen running in a state of panic from the entrance to Woodpark lodge, bumping into a lamppost, then recovering and running down the Dartry Road. He was shouting warnings to passers-by not to go down by Woodpark: 'There's a gun battle going on down there!' As a result of that gun battle Volunteer Timothy Coughlan lay dying outside the door of Woodpark lodge.

When calm was restored to the Redican household the family sat around the tiny kitchen table in silence, listening for the slightest sound that would indicate the attackers were still outside. The brothers worried how in God's name, with only one gun in the house – Harling's – they were going to defend themselves if the attackers decided to burst through the door. Thomas asked Harling, 'What the hell happened out there, Seán?'

Harling explained: 'I was followed home from Temple Road

by these two blokes who were on the far side of the road. When I reached the gates outside I looked over at them and saw that they had guns in their hands and were getting down into a firing position. I pulled out my own weapon and made a dive for the cover of the porch. Just as I did they fired a number of shots at me. I managed to get off a round myself before reaching cover. They came running across the road after me, firing their weapons as they came.

'Then suddenly all went quiet and the men disappeared. After a couple of minutes I popped my head up and peered out into the darkness to see if they were gone or if I could see where they were hiding. All of a sudden another round was fired at me and the flash blinded me for a couple of seconds. The bullet only missed me by half an inch.

'Then by sheer chance I saw this shadow coming towards me. I fired at it, then I opened the door. Just as I was closing it I heard someone running away from the gates.'

'And did you hit this shadow, Seán?' asked James, hoping he had.

'I don't know, Jim,' answered Harling, po-faced.

After four or five minutes elapsed and no further attack had come, Harling and Thomas ventured a peek outside. There they found the body of a man, hit by gunfire. Harling and James dragged the dying man inside while Thomas went to alert the police.

When the mother saw the body being carried in she turned her head and screamed, 'Oh my God! Oh my God! Oh my God!' Nora, upon seeing the body, also turned her head away, screamed 'Jesus Christ!' and drew her baby daughter close to her breast, protecting her from the sickening sight of the blood and brain matter that was oozing out of the poor man's head. She then ran to a corner in the tiny kitchen to be sick and very nearly vomited all over the child in her arms. They laid the man on the floor and Harling whispered an act of contrition into his ear.

Laurence was rushing about, full of nervous excitement and eager to know what he could do to help. James told him that he could go into the bedroom and sit with Father until it was all over, but he was not to tell him what was happening in the kitchen.

'Okay,' said Laurence. He was heading for the bedroom when James said, 'Hold on, Larry. You better take the baby with you.' Nora, doing her best to avoid stepping on the body on the floor while handing her now-hysterical child across it to Laurence, tripped and lost her balance. If it hadn't been for Laurence's agility and quick thinking the baby would surely have fallen on the body.

Laurence gripped the child firmly and brought her into the room, where he handed her to his father. The father cradled her lovingly in his arms, then asked, 'What in God's name is going on out there, Laurence?'

'It's better that you don't know, Father,' replied Laurence, fobbing him off.

Then the toing and froing began. The messenger boy from the Home and Colonial came, saw the body on the ground and went away; then, coming back to find the body gone, he left a parcel in the porch and went away again. The priests came and went – the mysterious priest first, then the sent-for priest. The police also came and went. Guns were handed over to them for inspection. Harling found the dying man's Fianna Fáil membership card in his pocket, and he was identified. James Redican remarked, 'Young Tim Coughlan, and I didn't recognise the poor lad when I knocked the cigarette butt out of his mouth.' Organised confusion reigned. And somewhere amid that confusion, Private Bartholomew Mooney of the Medical Corps in Portobello barracks received a telephone call at 7.20 p.m. from an unknown person, telling him, 'A man is dead at Woodpark lodge. Send out the ambulance.'

The ambulance, manned by Lieutenant Dr William Kerrigan of the Free State army and two orderlies from Portobello barracks, arrived at the gate lodge at 7.30 p.m. The doctor went to Coughlan and found him alive but unconscious, with a large hole in his head which was oozing blood and brain matter onto the kitchen floor. And without making a detailed examination, he concluded that the wound was fatal.

Kerrigan dressed the wound, then put the patient into the ambulance and brought him to the Meath hospital, where he was found to be dead on arrival. Timothy Coughlan had been left lying in agony on that cold kitchen floor for at least fifty minutes before he had received any sort of medical attention. Fianna Fáil/IRA had lost arguably one of their best, bravest and most loyal volunteers in the Dublin Brigade.

The ambulance had barely left the house when Superintendent O'Driscoll made the extraordinary decision that the scene of the shooting should be cleaned up. James Redican filled the bucket he had earlier thrown at Harling with water and washed away the blood and brain matter from the kitchen floor and from outside the door along with some spent cartridges. This saw all forensic evidence of the killing literally washed down the drain. And just as extraordinary, even though there were police of various ranks in Woodpark lodge for over an hour that night, was O'Driscoll's decision not to bother ordering even one of them to take a statement from any of the Redicans.

Laurence re-emerged from the bedroom with the baby in his arms just as Thomas arrived at the door and James had finished cleaning up the scene. The father remained in his room.

When Patrick arrived home from work at about 9.20 p.m. only the family was there, sitting around the table. All the police, including Harling, had gone. He sensed there was something wrong by the demeanour of the mother and his siblings and the negative atmosphere pervading the tiny dwelling. He asked the obvious question: 'Is there something wrong?'

His siblings looked at each other as much as to say, 'Which of us is going to tell him?' But the mother answered, 'There's been a shooting, Paddy.'

'A shooting!' he exclaimed. Then, looking at Nora and the baby, he asked, 'Where's Seán?'

The mother answered again: 'Seán was attacked on his way home from work tonight, Paddy, but he's all right. He shot and wounded his attacker but we think the poor man died afterwards. Seán is down in Pearse Street at the moment giving a statement.'

Patrick was very worried and he expressed his concern, saying, 'They will surely kill us all now.'

James tried to reassure him that they really had nothing to worry about and that all would be just fine. But Patrick was not reassured. 'I still think we're all goners,' he mumbled. He had a cup of tea and went to bed early but he hardly slept a wink all night.

The others stayed up until late, debating who could have called the ambulance out. They had no phone in their home, and the police had said it had not been them. Fianna Fáil, of course, later claimed that the phone call had been made from the detective branch at Pearse Street; they also denied having made it. So who was it? They never found out.

In the meantime, Harling was in Pearse Street garda station giving the investigating gardaí a detailed description of the second assailant. His superiors seemed to be in no doubt as to who that second man was. The hunt was on for Coughlan's accomplice and the home of the number-one suspect, Archie Doyle, at Ring Street, Inchicore, was raided that night by the Specials. Doyle was not at home.

The next morning, Sunday, the Redican home was once again under siege, this time by a posse of newspaper reporters. The reporters fired questions from all directions as each family member emerged from the house to attend mass in Rathgar. 'Was Harling wounded in the attack?' 'How come Coughlan's body ended up inside the lodge?' 'Was Harling really attacked at all?' 'Where exactly did the attack take place?' It was a frightening experience for them.

It had been reported in the Sunday-morning papers that a pool of blood on the road, which someone had covered with ashes, marked the spot where Coughlan fell. All through that afternoon groups of curious people came to inspect that spot, across the road from the gate lodge. They were trying to determine whether it really was blood or, as an official report stated, a large blob of oil left by a car that had parked there overnight. The Redicans watched them in wonderment.

Mrs Coughlan told the press that she had been on her way home from visiting a friend at about ten o'clock that night (implying that she hadn't heard about her son's death at that time) when she had met Thomas Kelly, a comrade of Timothy's from O'Donoghue Street, and that he had accompanied her home. When they had turned onto Ring Street they had seen a commotion going on outside number 42, Archie Doyle's house. She had hurried in to her husband to let him know that she was home and that she was going over to the Doyles' to find out what was going on. Her husband had told her that as far as he knew the police were looking for young Archie.

She and Thomas Kelly had gone over together. She had introduced herself to a detective and asked him what the raid was about. He had told her, rather callously, that she would know soon enough. Then he had arrested Thomas Kelly and detained him and her at the Doyles' until 1 a.m.

But word about Coughlan's killing had spread around other parts of the city and dozens of people, young and old, were already queuing to view his remains that night in the Meath hospital. It was from there Thomas Kelly was coming from when he met Mrs Coughlan along the road. If half the town knew about Coughlan's death, why didn't someone tell his parents?

Archie Doyle and his brother John were out when the raid on their home took place. They were more than likely also at the Meath hospital, viewing the remains of their fallen comrade and paying him their last respects. They returned at midnight and both they and Kelly were taken away to the Bridewell garda station, where they were grilled throughout the night. The Doyles' alibi, especially Archie's, stood up, because he had been in Coughlan's house, in conversation with his pal's father, at the very time the shooting had taken place out in Dartry. The Coughlans vouched for that. The Doyles were released early on Sunday afternoon and Kelly was released six hours later.

Timothy Coughlan's father, in a statement to the press, said that he was presented with a written report about his son's death at 2 a.m. on Sunday by a member of an garda síochána, and that that was the first the family had heard about it. In the same statement he said, 'I proceeded to the hospital immediately where I saw my son lying dead, with what appeared to be an entrance bullet wound near the centre of his forehead, and a big exit wound at the back.' Mrs Coughlan told them that she had been too grieved to visit the hospital.

Coughlan's remains were removed from the Meath hospital that Monday night and the hearse, flanked by a bodyguard of his young comrades, was led by the Éamon Ceannt pipe band. On Tuesday the remains were paraded slowly through the streets of Dublin on their way for internment in the republican plot in Glasnevin cemetery. The coffin was draped in the tricolour; again, the cortège was led by the Éamon Ceannt pipe band and the hearse flanked on either side by Coughlan's comrades from the IRA's Dublin Brigade.

The procession behind was led by his parents and siblings, the chief mourners. They in turn were followed by a contingent of Fianna Fáil deputies – Frank Aiken, Seán MacEntee, Seán Lemass, Seán T. O'Kelly, G. Boland, R. Briscoe, F. Kerlin, Éamon Cooney and M. O'Cleary. Walking in the main body of mourners were members of Cumann na mBan, Cumann na nGaedheal, Fianna Éireann, other nationalist organisations, trade unions, and the Women's Prisoners' Defence League, who brought a special wreath.

The graveside oration was delivered by Proinnsias Ó Riain, who stated that 'the enemies of Volunteer Coughlan had endeavoured to make his death one of dishonour', but that they, by their presence at his grave, had refuted that impression. 'Last Post' was sounded by a Fianna bugler.

James Redican, with some effrontery, attended Coughlan's funeral, but no one there challenged him. He was not threatened in any way, nor was he ignored. Some even came over and shook his hand. But despite all that, and even though it was made clear that they would not be targeted by the IRA, it was still a terribly frightening and dangerous period for the Redican family, especially for Thomas, who, it was rumoured, had played a part in the killing.

With Harling it was a different matter. He had gunned down a young IRA volunteer – one of their best – and that organisation was determined that he pay the full price for it.

Chapter 10

The Tribunal of Inquiry

The rider to the jury's verdict at the inquest was, 'We are of the opinion that the circumstances of the case should be a matter of further investigation.' This of course fuelled speculation that Coughlan had been murdered and not shot in self-defence. The Fianna Fáil organisation was furious; Deputies Frank Aiken, Seán Lemass and Seán MacEntee called for Seán Harling to be put on trial for his life. And the police whispered that because their own had failed to kill him, Fianna Fáil were now trying to get the state to do the job for them.

Fianna Fáil was painting the picture that Harling had murdered Coughlan in cold blood with the help of three of the Redican boys – Thomas, James and Laurence. They put forward the scenario that someone, probably Thomas Redican, had sneaked up on Coughlan, who had been sitting alone on the bench opposite their home enjoying a smoke, and had hit him on the head with a sandbag, rendering him unconscious. The unconscious Coughlan had been carried into the grounds of Woodpark lodge by the three Redicans and placed on the ground just a few feet away from the front door. There Harling had shot him through the back of the head. Afterwards, Harling had stage-managed the attack on himself and the lodge with the connivance of his three brothers-in-law. According to this version of events, Laurence Redican had been the man in the black coat seen running from Woodpark lodge.

They were determined to make Harling pay for his foul deed.

They proposed that the government set up a Dáil committee to investigate the killing, made up of selected sitting deputies from all parties. They expressed the belief that anything other than an independent Dáil investigation into the killing would be a 'whitewash'. But with Fianna Fáil's mind already made up that Harling was guilty of murder, and with the IRA wanting him dead, could their deputies sitting on that committee have given him a fair hearing? On 4 February 1928, an article calling for an independent investigation into the killing of Timothy Coughlan, written by Seán MacEntee, TD, appeared in the Fianna Fáil-backed newspaper *The Nation: A New Weekly Review*. At the end of that article MacEntee stated:

> In view of the past record of the Government, it is perhaps too much to hope that such an investigation will now be granted; but whether it is or not, this much is certain that when Fianna Fáil comes into power, the murder of Timothy Coughlan will not go unpunished.

Fianna Fáil did not get their independent Dáil investigation. Instead a tribunal of inquiry met in public at the city hall, Dublin, on 27 February 1928 and for seven days during the month of March.

Counsels for an garda síochána, Mr Bewley, SC, Mr Lavery, SC, and E. J. Kelly, BL, instructed by the chief state solicitor, presented forty-one witnesses. One was presented by counsel for the Fianna Fáil organisation, Conor Maguire, BL, instructed by Messrs Little, Ó hUadhaigh and Proud solicitors. Two witnesses were presented by counsels for Timothy Coughlan's next of kin, J. O'Connor, SC, and A. Lynn, BL, instructed by P. Campbell, solicitor. One witness appeared for Special Intelligence Officer Seán Harling, whom J. Fitzgerald, SC, and T. Finlay, BL, instructed by Mr Norman, solicitor, represented.

A special extra day's sitting was held at the Metropolitan District Court, Inns Quay, on 29 March to accommodate one witness, a Mrs Carter. The total number of witnesses examined was forty-six.

The minister for justice, James Fitzgerald-Kenny, appointed George P. Cussen, senior justice of the Metropolitan District Court, as chairman. He was assisted by two justices of the District Court – Cyril J. Beatty and Seán Treo. Stanislaus Flanagan was appointed as registrar.

The rider to the jury's verdict from the inquest had been drawn from the evidence given by Dr Wilfred Lane. But at the tribunal, Dr William Boxwell explained that the fracture on the left side of Coughlan's head had not been caused by an independent blow by sandbag or any other instrument and that all the fractures had been caused by a single bullet. Dr Lane then retracted the statement he made at the inquest and concurred with Dr Boxwell's hypothesis.

Dr Boxwell was professor of pathology in the College of Surgeons and a fellow of the College of Physicians. He was also attached to the Meath hospital and had performed the post-mortem on Coughlan's body alongside Dr Lane that night. He had not been called by Coroner Byrne to give evidence at the inquest. Dr Boxwell agreed with Dr Lane that Coughlan had been shot from behind and at close quarters.

When Harling's cross-examination began Mr O'Connor, counsel for the Coughlan family, lunged straight in where he had left off at the inquest, trying to find out when Harling had joined the secret service.

'Were you in the Detective Department when you burgled the Fianna Éireann offices in Drury Street in 1927?'

Mr Bewley, counsel for an garda síochána, objected, saying that he had instructions from the head of Harling's department to claim privilege for any question put as to the period of service or duties performed by him in the intelligence service. Mr O'Connor demanded to know on what legal grounds Mr Bewley was putting his claim for privilege. The chairman pointed out that it had already been given in evidence by an intelligence officer that Harling was a member of the intelligence forces.

'Before your worship rules,' said O'Connor, 'I want to be very specific on this. The head of a department can claim privilege for certain things which are set out in every textbook on evidence. Counsel has no right to claim privilege, at all, whether he represents the head of the state or whether he does not.'

O'Connor, backed up by Mr Maguire, counsel for Fianna Fáil, demanded that the head of the department be summoned to attend the inquiry.

The chairman said, 'As we understand it, you wish the head of the department to be here to explain why he claims privilege for this witness.'

'Yes,' replied O'Connor. 'My cross-examination will largely depend on that answer.'

'Very well,' said the chairman.

That afternoon Henry O'Friel, head of the Department of Justice, was sworn in. He told the tribunal that he had been instructed by the minister for justice to claim privilege on any question about the secret service or its agents that was not relevant to this case.

Then, after long and tedious legal argument, the chairman gave his ruling.

'We are agreed that we are bound by the evidence given by the principal officer of this department, who says that in his opinion to answer that question would be prejudicial to the public interest. We are agreed that Seán Harling is not bound to answer the question put to him by Mr O'Connor.'

And so Fianna Fáil, right from the start of the tribunal, had set out their stall. Deputy Ernest Blythe accused Deputy Seán Lemass and Fianna Fáil of being more interested in the facts and circumstances of Seán Harling's employment in the state's secret service than in the facts and circumstances surrounding the death of Timothy Coughlan.

But Fianna Fáil was determined to find out when exactly Harling had turned – if only to determine what damage done to their organisation, and to Fianna Éireann, between July 1926 and August 1927 they could lay at his door. They also wished to eliminate the possibility of other spies in the camp. Therefore, counsels for Fianna Fáil and the Coughlan family concentrated their cross-examination of Harling on trying to extract from him, through very clever questioning, how long he had been a special detective. It did not work. They tried the same tactics while cross-examining the Redicans but failed because the Redicans, like Harling, were wise to them.

O'Connor caused uproar when he insinuated that Harling had put the Fianna Fáil membership card in Coughlan's pocket: 'It was conveniently found there,' he said. He was forced to withdraw the remark and apologise to the court (though it is true that volunteers, when out on certain assignments, would be instructed not to carry any form of identification).

Harling's cross-examination by counsels for Fianna Fáil and the Coughlans was intense. He caved in at one stage under a barrage of questioning and admitted that he had been caretaking a substantial arms dump for the Dublin Brigade of the IRA while he was working as an intelligence officer for the state. The lawyers were trying to show the tribunal and the Department of Justice that Harling was a man of dubious nature and therefore could not be trusted or believed by either side.

Of course, O'Connor and Maguire did not know that Harling had laid down certain conditions before joining the Specials. And he had earlier denied, under the same type of pressure, that he had ever been Countess Markievicz's chauffeur, when the whole world and its mother knew that he had been and continued to be after joining the secret service. He even lied to the tribunal about the date he resigned from the Fianna. So why had he admitted that he had been a caretaker of an IRA arms dump at the same time as he was working as a special detective?

His superiors were aware of the terms and conditions they had agreed to before he joined them, but none of those conditions included being allowed to mind IRA dumps while he was working for them without turning in the arms and personnel involved. By admitting to caretaking that particular dump, Harling was practically confirming the double-agent theory for those within government and the Specials who had never trusted him in the first place.

Up next for a scalding cross-examination were the Redicans. The hostility shown to them by counsels for Fianna Fáil and the Coughlans was plain to see. The lawyers were seeking to prove to the tribunal that the Redicans had colluded with Harling in the killing of Timothy Coughlan. They did their best to blacken the Redicans' names and characters by portraying them as liars, cheats and scoundrels. This would plant in the minds of the three judges a seed of doubt about their reliability as witnesses. But the Redicans proved to be more than a match for them.

The first of the Redicans to be examined was Tom. O'Connor,

counsel for the Coughlans, became infuriated when he asked him whether it had disturbed the equanimity of the Redican family that shots were being fired outside their window.

Thomas answered, 'No, they are used to that.'

'What do you mean by that?' O'Connor fumed.

'We are used to scraps,' replied Redican calmly. 'I was out in 1916 and my brother was out.' Thomas was enjoying rubbing it in.

'Were you in the post office?' asked a cynical O'Connor.

'I was in Boland's mill. I was sent over on the Tuesday evening with a dispatch from Mr de Valera to Mrs de Valera. He told me not to return, that I was too young.'

'You were not in any of the "scraps" in 1921 anywhere?' asked Mr O'Connor, again with a cynical air.

Redican looked at him in bewilderment, and then answered, 'How could I have been? Don't you know I was in prison from 1921 onwards? But I was in many a little scrap afterwards.'

O'Connor, making no effort to disguise his hostility towards Redican, put it to him that he had boasted about the killing of Timothy Coughlan to his fellow soldiers in the canteen in the Catholic home in the Curragh camp. Redican replied that that was absolutely untrue but that he had been asked questions about it, which he had refused to answer.

O'Connor, clearly annoyed, asked him if he knew a man named Laurence Flynn and another named John Keogh, both of whom worked in the canteen in the Catholic home. He replied that he did not.

'Did you ever tell them that you were in trouble over a man in Dublin, that you had knocked him down, and that your brother-in-law, Seán Harling, had shot him dead?' said O'Connor in a loud voice.

Redican gave an emphatic, 'No, sir.'

'Of course, this is not the first time the police have taken a statement from you,' O'Connor sarcastically remarked.

'This is the first time,' replied Redican, sternly.

'I am not talking about statements in this case only, Mr Redican. I am talking about them taking a statement from you back on 10 May 1921 when they arrested you for a bank raid,' said O'Connor in an agitated manner.

'The police take a statement from me? Never,' replied Redican, again sternly.

That cross-examination ended. Laurence Flynn and John Keogh were not called by counsel to give evidence backing the statement they had allegedly given to O'Connor about what Thomas Redican had allegedly said in the Curragh camp.

When Laurence Redican was called to the stand it did not go unnoticed by Mr Lynn, counsel for the Coughlan family, that he happened to be wearing a black cloth overcoat.

'Mr Redican, how long have you had the black overcoat you are now wearing?' asked Lynn.

'I think I've had it some months.'

'So you had it on 28 January?'

'Yes, I had.'

Lynn went on to ask questions about the more humdrum details of that night, like who was sitting where, who was reading what paper, and so on. But from his first two questions he left an obvious air of insinuation floating around the courtroom.

Mr Fitzgerald, counsel for Seán Harling, set about clearing the particular air.

'You were asked about this black overcoat you are wearing,' he said to Laurence. 'Do you know why?'

'No, except that it might be said that I had stolen it.'

'The suggestion was that you were the man wearing a black overcoat who got away from these premises and was seen running towards Orwell Park …' said Fitzgerald.

'No,' replied Redican. 'I wasn't out.'

'… and who ran against a lamp, but took up his steps and disappeared in the darkness,' Fitzgerald continued.

'No.'

'You didn't bring this black overcoat today to make it an exhibit in the case?'

'No.'

When O'Connor and Maguire began cross-examining James Redican they began to try and discredit him as an unreliable witness. O'Connor first gave him a severe grilling about the bank raids back in 1921. Then, at the end of that questioning, he said dismissively, 'So much for your previous history.' When Redican said, 'You are forgetting to ask for my associates in these bank raids,' O'Connor retorted angrily, 'I am not forgetting anything.'

Then, after Redican had told the hearing that he had seen Seán Harling's gun when he had showed it to his superior officers in the house, O'Connor cleverly continued the smear campaign.

'Did you examine your brother-in-law's gun?' he asked.

'No,' said James.

'Of course, you know a good deal about guns.'

'Something.'

'You have made some use of them in your time?'

'For Irish freedom.'

'For filling your own pockets, too?' O'Connor insisted.

'What do you mean by that?'

'Bank robberies.'

'Not my own pockets,' said James angrily. 'The pockets of the Irish Republican Army.'

O'Connor changing tactics for the moment.

'You are not working?' he said.

'I am unemployed.'

'As Redican you are unemployed,' said O'Connor, 'but you are sometimes employed as Casey?'

'It is not a permanent job.'

'The name Casey is only *pro tem*?'

'Yes.'

'Do you still use it?'

'No, sir.'

'What name do you use now?'

'Seamus Ó Roideacháin.'

'Is that your private inquiry agency name?' O'Connor was reminding the court about Redican having been charged with impersonating a police officer in 1927.

'I haven't been doing private inquiry work for some time.'

O'Connor then suddenly returned to the line of questioning about Redican's knowledge of guns, hoping that it would prove more damaging to his credibility. But Redican was fit for him. O'Connor asked a tricky question.

'Do you remember a man named Fox being murdered at Orwell Park last September?'

'I don't remember, but I know that he was murdered.'

'What did you do with your gun?' said O'Connor.

'Which gun?' asked James.

'The last gun you had.'

'During the British fighting?'

'Oh no, much later than that.'

'I hadn't a gun since that.'

'What did you do with the last gun you had?'

'The last gun I had was in February 1921.'

'What became of that?'

'It was dumped.'

'You have never had a gun since?'

'No.'

'You never handled a gun since February 1921?'

'No.'

'You have seen one, of course?'

'Dozens of them.'

'You never had one since?' asked O'Connor for a third time.

'Never had one in my hand.'

'You have been a man of peace since?'

'Considering that I am a man of pieces, suffering from wounds received fighting for Irish freedom, I ought to be a man of peace,' said Redican.

O'Connor then gave way to his colleague, Conor Maguire, who immediately got stuck into Redican about the bank raids. He was determined to show the tribunal that the raids had never been sanctioned by the IRA, and the fact that Redican recognised the court at that time was further proof that the raids had been unofficial and of a criminal nature. He was hoping that by the end of his cross-examination the minds of the three judges would be imbued with the idea that Redican was a scoundrel and incapable of telling the truth.

'Mr James Cawley, instructed by Mr P. H. O'Brien, appeared for you?' Maguire began.

'Yes,' replied Redican.

'You didn't refuse to recognise the court?'

'No, not at that time.'

'Though it was May 1921?'

'At that time I had to recognise it.'

'Do you suggest that members of the IRA at that time, unless on trial for their lives, were bound to recognise the court?'

'Yes. I was being charged with a criminal offence and it was necessary for me to be defended by counsel. At that time there was also a suggestion about the shooting of Auxiliaries, which carried the death penalty. I had to be represented by counsel.'

'Until you heard of the sum of five thousand pounds at the court-martial proceedings you didn't know what had been seized?'

'Yes.'

'You were responsible to the officer of the IRA for the amount of money seized?'

'No, I was responsible for the seizing of it and handing it over to the brigadier.'

'You say the money was never counted?'

'No, it was locked in an attaché case as it was seized by Weymes and Murray and handed over to T. J. Burke in Mullingar. I was the man with the gun, in charge of the men, and I had to see that they got away.'

'Wasn't everything you did official?'

'Not everything, but things done unofficially were afterwards made official.'

'Does that mean that these bank raids were not official, but were sanctioned officially?'

'There were things that happened in Claremorris, Mr Maguire, that were unofficial, and they were afterwards claimed to be official.'

'They were sanctioned?' asked the chairman.

'Yes,' said James.

Try as he might, Maguire could not trip Redican up, but he made one last gasp effort to discredit him.

'I suggest to you that whatever may be the truth regarding the events of the night of 28 January, the story you have told here today is untrue,' he said.

'I suppose what you want to say is that in the case of poor Coughlan they are trying to deny that he went to shoot Harling as they tried to deny that I was on official bank raids.'

'You were prepared for my question?'

'Undoubtedly.'

'You were prepared for the suggestion that the story is a concocted story?'

'It is the truth.'

'You were quite prepared for the question?'

'I am prepared for anything you want to throw at me.'

'Do you mean to say you are prepared for being accused of committing perjury?'

'I am speaking the truth, and when speaking the truth I am prepared for any question.'

James Redican was then cross-examined by Mr Fitzgerald, counsel for Seán Harling.

'You have been asked a number of questions about these raids, and you mentioned about two men engaged. Was one Thomas Weymes?' asked Fitzgerald.

'Yes,' said James.

'And was he convicted at the same time as you?'

'Yes.'

'And was he sentenced to twelve years' penal servitude and twelve strokes of the cat? Did either of you get that?'

'No.'

'Was he released with you?'

'Yes.'

'Was there also a man named William Murray engaged in these raids?'

'Yes, sir.'

'Is he still a leading official in Fianna Fáil?'

'Yes, he has been organising in the midlands. He was wounded in the last war.'

'Both himself and Weymes were Irregulars?'

'Yes.'

'He is at present in the Fianna Fáil organisation?'

'Yes.'

'Where is he at present?'

'In the midlands, organising,' James repeated.

'What is the purpose of these questions?' interjected the chairman. 'How is it to the credit of the witness?'

'To show that they were engaged in official raids,' said Fitzgerald.

'My friend has made suggestions about a man named Murray, who was concerned in these raids with this man,' ventured Maguire. 'I suggest that Murray was not tried by court martial.'

'Was Murray tried?' asked Mr Beatty, one of the judges.

'No, but he was on the bank raids,' replied Redican.

Fitzgerald continued, 'Was there also a man named James Murray?' Maguire objected immediately. 'I am now showing,' said Fitzgerald, 'that this witness and several members of Mr Maguire's own organisation were engaged in a laudable national enterprise.' To Redican he said, 'Was a man named James Gaffney, who was not captured, engaged with you?'

'Yes,' James replied.

'And Christopher Fitzsimons?'

'Yes.'

'And Michael Murray?'

'Yes.'

'Acting under orders of your superior officer in Mullingar?'

'Yes.'

'And most of them are still identified with Fianna Fáil?'

'Yes. Michael Murray, Christopher Fitzsimons and William Murray are still with Fianna Fáil.'

Maguire interrupted, 'None of these men whose names have been mentioned were tried with you?'

'No, except Weymes. He got twelve years.'

'Then, except for your word,' continued Maguire, 'there is not a tittle of evidence to connect these men with the raids?'

'I can produce you the evidence.'

That answer ended the cross-examination of James Redican. Surprisingly, given how counsel for Fianna Fáil seemed determined to brand Redican as a devious liar, they did not invite any of the above-named members of their party to take the stand to refute Redican's allegations about them.

Joseph Reynolds, called and examined by Mr Lynn for the Coughlan family, confirmed that he had been secretary to Fianna Éireann for a number of years and had been chief scoutmaster for all of Dublin, but that he had resigned from that organisation. He was then cross-examined by Mr Bewley for an garda síochána.

Bewley began: 'Do you consider that a person leaving your organisation and joining other organisations would be a traitor and deserve to meet a traitor's fate?'

'I have not considered what fate he [meaning Harling] should

meet but any man who swore an oath of allegiance to the republic and then swore something to a lesser authority is a traitor.'

That statement immediately landed Reynolds in trouble. He
had fallen into Bewley's trap, for he had resigned from the Fianna
and joined Fianna Fáil. Was the pot calling the kettle black?

'I suppose,' continued Bewley, 'in your opinion the worst kind
of traitor would be a man who belonged to Fianna Éireann at
one time and then went over to the Free State government?'

Reynolds, realising the blunder he had made in the answer to
the previous question, became aware of where Mr Bewley was trying to lead him. He answered, tongue in cheek, 'Traitor to what?'

Bewley had him on the run. Holding up a copy of the Fianna
Éireann constitution, he said, 'I ask you whether persons who in
the words of this document "blindly followed leaders who had
themselves gone wrong" are traitors.'

Reynolds, evading the question, answered, 'Is it my opinion
you want?'

'Would he be in your opinion a traitor?' asked Bewley.

Reynolds, again answered, 'I would leave these people to Pro-
vidence.'

Bewley pressed and pressed Reynolds for an answer that would
leave him with egg on his face. But Reynolds hummed and hawed,
stuttered and fumbled until the chairman of the tribunal, Mr G.
P. Cussen, came to his rescue and instructed Bewley not to force
the witness to answer. Bewley, satisfied that he had made his point,
answered, 'Very well. I will not press the question further.'

Poor Joseph Reynolds had been pushed to the edge of a cliff
by the clever Mr Bewley. How could he answer Bewley's clever
question without directly implying that he and the other militants – including Timothy Coughlan, who had resigned from

the Fianna to join Fianna Fáil – were themselves traitors? That would imply, indeed, that all those others who had left Sinn Féin and other republican organisations to join Fianna Fáil deserved a traitor's fate. Fianna Fáil's leader, Éamon de Valera, along with all that party's sitting TDs, was clearly perceived to have 'gone wrong' because he had signed the oath of allegiance to a lesser authority, the king of England. Joseph Reynolds, it would seem, had no choice but to resist the urge to brand Seán Harling a traitor for going over to the Free State, lest he fall off the cliff.

But Reynolds was not off the hook yet. He was pressed on the same subject when cross-examined by Mr Fitzgerald, and his answers to Fitzgerald's questions were just as evasive as his answers to Bewley's had been.

'If a man left Fianna Éireann,' Fitzgerald began, 'and instead of joining the IRA, he desired to join a detective force, what would Fianna Éireann think of him? Would he be called a spy and a traitor?'

'It is a matter for himself if he leaves Fianna Éireann,' said Reynolds.

'If he became an adherent of the Free State government and a member of their detective force to spy on Fianna Éireann, would he not become a traitor to the republic? If he became subservient to the republic [Free State] …'

Mr Lynn for the Coughlan family interjected: 'I am objecting to this question because Mr Bewley did not give evidence that Harling did join the detective force on such a date, or that he did so to spy on Fianna Éireann. Evidence must be given as to that.' They were still trying to find out when exactly Harling had joined the Specials.

Bewley continued: 'If he did both these things, was he not

false to the ideal of an Irish republic? And, in addition to that, he became a member of a detective force to spy on former companions. What fate does he deserve from the hands of a faithful member of the Irish republic?'

'Why do you ask me that? Is it in the hope that you will get an opinion?' Fitzgerald was hoping that Reynolds would answer yes, so he could go on to try and prove that Fianna Fáil was the political wing of the IRA, who had sentenced Harling to death.

'I only want the truth. What do you think should be done with such a man?'

'Leave him in the hands of God.'

'I take it from that answer that you belong to the non-militant party?'

'You can take it as you like.'

Reynolds held fast in his refusal to give direct answers to the questions posed to him by counsels for Harling and the police.

In Coughlan's father's short evidence to the tribunal he stated that, at about six o'clock on the evening of the shooting, a pal of Timothy's named Doyle called to the house looking for him, saying he had an appointment to meet him there at that time. Coughlan's father, it seems, was further crystallising Doyle's rock-solid alibi. If he had been in Coughlan's house at six o'clock that night how could he have been sitting on a seat miles away on the Dartry Road with Timothy Coughlan before 6.35 p.m., waiting to attack Seán Harling?

Having carefully examined and considered all the facts put before them the three members of the tribunal presented their findings to the minister for justice. As expected, Harling was exonerated:

On these facts the tribunal are satisfied: that Timothy Coughlan referred to in the Order of the Minister for Justice dated the 15th day of February 1928, was killed by a bullet fired by Seán Harling from a Webley .45 revolver and that Seán Harling fired the shot on an occasion when he was being attacked by Timothy Coughlan and another man, and that this shot was fired by Harling, after shots had been fired at him with intent to kill by Timothy Coughlan.

Seán Harling, Private Redican, and James Redican were each subjected to severe and searching cross-examination. The tribunal could find no reason to doubt the truth of their evidence with reference to the subject matter of the inquiry. Mrs Harling was in a delicate state of health [pregnant]. Her recollection of what happened on the evening of 28 January 1928, was not very accurate for that reason. She was not subjected to a very severe cross-examination. The tribunal believe she was telling the truth to the best of her recollection. The other members of the Redican family gave answers when under cross-examination which in the opinion of the tribunal were deliberately untruthful. Nothing elicited from these witnesses when under cross-examination affected the findings of the tribunal.

Counsel for an garda síochána in opening the proceedings before the tribunal referred to rumours circulated in the city, newspaper articles making charges against certain persons, and to the Rider of the Jury to their verdict at the Coroner's Inquest on the body of Timothy Coughlan, with a view to showing why this tribunal was appointed. The tribunal consider that the jury at the Coroner's Inquest on the body of Timothy Coughlan were justified in adding the Rider to their verdict, and that the grounds were afforded for some of the rumours circulated by the following circumstances:

(a) The evidence adduced at the coroner's inquest was not exhaustive.

It was suggested at the inquest that some of the injuries received by Timothy Coughlan was [sic] caused by a blow from a sandbag. The medical evidence produced before the tribunal as already stated showed clearly:

That all Timothy Coughlan's injuries were caused by a bullet,

No injury could have been caused by a blow from a sandbag or other implement.

(b) Great stress was laid, at the inquest, on the fact that the bullet which killed Timothy Coughlan entered at the back of his head.

The tribunal have found that Timothy Coughlan was killed by a bullet fired by Seán Harling, immediately after Timothy Coughlan had fired his last shot. They believe that Timothy Coughlan, after firing his last shot, turned to get away and so received Harling's bullet in the back of the head.

It was widely believed, especially by Fianna Fáil supporters, that the outcome of the tribunal of inquiry was a foregone conclusion. Harling's name was going to be cleared. After all, his version of events of that fateful Saturday night was the only show in town. There was no witness they could call to contradict his evidence, save for the man in the dark coat. And that character was not going to take the stand to state that Harling's account of what happened was false, running the risk of getting himself arrested and charged with the serious crime of attempting to kill a police officer – which carried with it the death penalty.

The question remained, though, as to whether Fianna Fáil, because they could not produce any proof of police complicity in the killing (which they had hoped to do), concocted the version of events they were portraying – the insinuation that the whole Redican family conspired with Harling to kill Coughlan.

After the tribunal Fianna Fáil, Fianna Éireann and the IRA still were unsure how much damage Harling's intelligence work had done to their organisations. Doubt about some of the discoveries made by the Specials lingered in their minds because they just did not know when or why Harling had turned his coat, or whether there were more spies in the camp. Because they had no other suspect, they credited him with most of their misfortunes since July 1926, and so decided that he had to die for 'going wrong'.

Meanwhile, some government ministers and some Specials had had the idea that Harling was a double agent. They had expressed their suspicions to Neligan and O'Duffy, who at first ignored them. They themselves developed doubts about the authenticity of Harling's information, however, after a couple houses they raided for arms turned out to be clean and their occupants apolitical. O'Friel and O'Connell were never happy with what Harling had given them. They suspected that all the while he had been supplying them with minnows and the big fish had been getting away. Now, after hearing evidence at the tribunal of inquiry that Harling had been minding an arms dump for the IRA while he was working for the state, they felt vindicated in their distrust of him and decided that his attachment to the Specials should be guillotined.

Apparently Harling was still of some use to them, however, for his attachment remained, and armed detectives were assigned to protect him on a 24-hour rota basis. Some refused to do it and those who did, did so reluctantly.

Harling was costing the state money now and manpower that they couldn't afford. In August he was called in to Finian O'Driscoll's office once more, where O'Driscoll, O'Duffy, Neligan and O'Friel threw a fresh scare into him. They informed him that they had new intelligence that the IRA had, once again, assembled a small band of volunteers with specific orders to kill him on sight. They compounded that bad news by telling him they were withdrawing his police protection. This was a devastating blow to Harling. He vigorously protested, stating that he was an officer in the Free State secret service and that it was their sworn duty to provide protection for fellow officers in predicaments such as his. But they did not want to hear his protestations. They just wanted rid of him.

O'Duffy bluntly told him, 'Look, Seán, we just can't afford the time or the manpower and that's that.' And O'Friel took back the gun he had given him for self-protection, saying, 'We can no longer defend your life, Seán, so we are advising you to leave the country immediately. Stay away for a few years or until we deem it safe for you to return. Then you will get your civil-service job back.'

Harling pleaded, 'Jaysus, at least leave me with my gun. It's bad enough that you're throwing me to the wolves, but you could at least give me back my gun to help defend myself and my family from attack.' But there was no moving O'Friel or O'Duffy.

So, after having joined the Free State secret service in June 1926 to spy on Fianna Éireann, Harling's usefulness to the state came to a swift end. Suspecting him of being a double agent, they severed all ties. They offered him some subsistence money and told him to leave the country, hoping that he would settle somewhere, send for his wife and family and never again return.

Harling was now a lonely fearful man, afraid to venture outside his own hall door lest he be shot dead. He did not even have the comfort of the protection of his brother-in-law, for back in June James Redican had written to the Department of Justice asking that he be relieved of the obligation to report to the police. The Prisons Board had strongly objected, reminding the Department of Justice that they still regarded Redican as a clever and most dangerous individual who, if a suitable opportunity presented itself, would again engage in crime:

> Despite the fact that his conduct in the past year has been good, we are strongly of the opinion that the obligation of reporting to the police should not for the present be remitted … It must be remembered that this man was, this time last year, convicted at the Dublin district court for unlawfully assuming the rank and designation of an officer of an garda.

The department were awaiting a report from the Riverstown gardaí before they could furnish James with a verdict. But James did not wait. He secretly boarded the mail boat for Holyhead and headed for London, where he found work as a gentleman's valet using the name Riordan. He retained that name and later married under it.

James Redican's disappearance greatly alarmed the police, who immediately assumed he was planning to commit a crime of some sort with others, and that those others could well be the IRA. They scoured the country looking for him. Of course, none of the Redicans knew of his whereabouts.

When the police finally discovered that he was working in London they turned a blind eye and reported their discovery to the Prisons Board on 26 July: 'We understand he has obtained work there.' They left him alone and he never again returned to Dublin or to the land he had fought and almost died for.

Towards the end of August 1928, Harling was feeling the strain of living with his in-laws in hiding and the worry that he was putting them, his child and his wife (who was pregnant again) in serious danger. Believing that it would not be long now before the IRA would come for him, an embittered Seán Harling reluctantly took the money offered him by the state and left for Canada (not America as some reports have stated), taking with him the youngest Redican boy, Laurence (not, according to my father and my uncle Thomas, his wife and child, as the same reports contend).

Chapter 11

Pining for His Family

Seán Harling did not like being away from home. He missed his wife and two children. He found living in a foreign country difficult and costly and it was not long before he found himself on his uppers again. His pining for home and his family got the better of him and, after being hardly a year away, he left Canada and arrived in London in November 1929, where he found accommodation in the Queensgate area of south Kensington.

Laurence Redican did not return with him, choosing instead to cross the border into the USA, where he found work as a motor mechanic. He settled in the Flatbush area of Brooklyn, New York, where he met and married a girl from Tourmekeady, County Mayo. They reared two boys, Kevin and Larry. He became one of the father figures of Irish traditional music in New York and was a founder member of the New York céilí band. He played both the fiddle and the banjo. He died aged sixty-six, after suffering a heart attack while playing his beloved music on stage in New York on 26 January 1975.

In early January 1930, Seán Harling wrote to Diarmuid O'Hegarty, secretary of Dáil Éireann, expressing a wish to return to the Free State as he was anxious to be with his wife and children. He also asked:

> Would you be kind enough to help me secure from the Civil Service Commission a job, on the plea that I am a suspended Civil Servant since 1922. I know I am entitled to a hearing on suspension grounds and can prove I am not a member of the IRA. Thanking you for favourable reply.
>
> Yours,
> John Harling

Why would Harling feel obliged to tell O'Hegarty that he could prove to the Civil Service Commission that he was not in the IRA? It seems that he thought certain elements among the Free State authorities still believed that he had been a double agent.

O'Hegarty replied on 1 February, writing, 'Unfortunately I am extremely busy at present and it may be some little time before I can write to you fully.' Unbeknown to O'Hegarty and the police, however, Harling had already slipped back into the country a few days before O'Hegarty's letter arrived in London and was living at Woodpark lodge. The letter was forwarded to him there.

O'Hegarty sent a copy of Harling's letter to Henry O'Friel, secretary to the Department of Justice, with a note attached, which read, 'I doubt if it will be possible to arrange his reinstatement, but before taking the matter up, I shall be glad to know if you desire to make any observations.' O'Hegarty knew that O'Friel had never trusted Harling. Perhaps he was really hoping O'Friel might confirm his belief that Harling was suspected of being a double agent. O'Friel did make an observation. He wrote:

> In my judgement Harling has no further claims. He was treated generously enough and many another man had to make a fresh start under worse conditions and it was unreasonable for him

to return. It is no excuse that he found other countries too difficult or too costly. The police can scarcely be expected to regard Harling's return as anything but inconvenient. He is of no use to them and his life cannot be said to be safe. I don't see how he could get state employment.

In the meantime, Harling wrote to the inquiry committee into the cases of dismissed civil servants set up by the minister for finance in 1928. He learned that Diarmuid O'Hegarty's brother was on that committee and managed to secure an interview with him and a promise of help.

Harling also wrote to Colm Ó Murchadha, clerk of the Dáil, who passed the letter on to the committee, adding a footnote: 'Perhaps Micheál Ó Loingsigh would be able to let us have some information as to the circumstances of his suspension.' Ó Loingsigh sent a note to Ó Murchadha on 5 February, reminding him that 'acting on your instructions, I informed him early in July 1922 that his services were no longer required'.

On 8 February, Diarmuid O'Hegarty was directed by the committee of inquiry to inform Colm Ó Murchadha that Harling had applied to them requesting his old job as clerk in the Dáil secretariat back:

> The Committee would be glad if you could verify Mr Harling's statements as set out above and furnish them with a full report as to the circumstances in which his services in your department were terminated. It would also be appreciated if you would indicate whether Mr Harling's services from the point of view of ordinary official discipline were satisfactory during the period of his employment.

> Diarmuid O'Hegarty

Colm Ó Murchadha wrote to the committee on 11 February:

> A Chara,
> I enclose copy of note from Mr Ó Loingsigh regarding the termination of the services of Seán Harling. I should say that Mr Ó Loingsigh's recollection is correct and that the reason for Harling's dismissal was his association with the Irregular Forces operating at that time. My own recollection of Harling is that he was a good lad and that his services were satisfactory from the point of view of ordinary official discipline.
>
> Mise le meas,
> Colm Ó Murchadha

On one front, then, Harling's future was beginning to look bright and sunny with the prospect of him being reinstated in the civil service. But on another front he might not have a future at all – the threat of assassination by the IRA still hung over him. He was wary of every stranger, especially those wearing soft hats and fawn-coloured trenchcoats, approaching him on the street, because he had been verbally abused several times while out and about. He had received numerous threats telling him that he was a goner and even had the odd punch thrown at him at Fianna Éireann functions and commemorations.

As if the threat on his life from the IRA was not enough for him to contend with, those elements within the Free State government who considered him a thorn in their side and wanted him extracted started a campaign of intimidation and harassment against him. They put obstacle after obstacle in the way of his being reinstated in the civil service. They even recruited senior police officers to help them, going as far as getting them to threaten him. People whose ear he had at one time began to ignore him, including the two men who had tried to recruit him into spying for the state in the first place, and in whom he had great hope – Diarmuid O'Hegarty and Richard Mulcahy.

Harling called to O'Hegarty's office a few times but O'Hegarty was always too busy to see him. His ex-police colleagues did not want him around either, opening up old wounds, so they enthusiastically joined their superiors and ministerial masters in intimidating him.

Harling feared state agents as much as the IRA. But what really scared him – and what drove him to believe that he was being set up by state agents to be killed by the IRA – was a visit one night by General Eoin O'Duffy, commissioner of police.

When push came to shove, Harling took what he believed was the only option open to him. He wrote to Diarmuid O'Hegarty on 27 February 1930:

Dear Diarmuid,

I tried to see you twice last week, but failed, the matter I wanted to see you on was, re suspension.

I was informed by the commissioner of police that my application for reinstatement was rejected, that I could not carry arms, all protection withdrawn, and that I could not reside in Dublin. I cannot understand this victimisation as I committed no crime against the state, and something should be done if they want me to go, as I am sure a job of some kind could be found for me in London, instead of turning me out of my home without any way of living or providing for my wife and children.

Now I am prepared to go and give an undertaken [sic] not to return if a job is found for me, and I am sure this could be easily arranged as it was done many times before, for others.

I hope you will find time to reply at once before any further action is taken against me.

Thanking you for favourable reply.

Yours Respectfully,
Seán Harling

P.S. Maybe you have some business friends in London that you could recommend me to?

On 3 March, after one long, anxious and nerve-racking week for Harling, O'Hegarty replied:

A chara,

I am sorry that you missed me when you came to the office last week, but I was very busy.

I understood when you left for abroad that your departure was facilitated so that you might not be subjected to any inconvenience or risk arising out of the prominence into which you came. Your return was of your own free will, and I find it hard to see, having regard to what has already been done for you, that your return was reasonable or how you can expect anything more to be done for you now.

If I knew of anybody in London who would be in a position to get you a post I should be very glad to do anything I could, but unfortunately my acquaintances in London are not business people, and I cannot at the moment think of anybody who would be in a position to help you as a result of my intervention.

Mise, le meas,
Diarmuid O'Hegarty

At last, the Free State authorities were washing their hands of Harling completely, sending him off to drift alone on an ocean of fear and intimidation and a future of uncertainty. Still not allowed to carry a gun, and the police refusing to protect him, he had absolutely no defence against attack and no means of earning a living. In the letter from O'Hegarty, who had been told by Henry O'Friel that the Free State were unwilling to help Harling in any way, not even by getting him a job in London, he had had it straight from the horse's mouth.

While thinking long and hard about his predicament he pondered certain questions. Why would the committee tell the commissioner of police to inform him that they had rejected his application for reinstatement? Why did they not write to him directly? Perhaps, thought Harling, his application was not rejected at all and they were still considering it. And if that was so, did it not mean that the element in government who wanted rid of him had recruited the commissioner of police to their side and used him to try to force him out of the country? Another thing he could not understand was why all his old buddies were steering clear of him and his situation.

Harling believed the state owed him. They had promised him his old job as clerk in the civil service back when he returned and he was now calling for that promise to be honoured. He did not consider this simple request unreasonable. After all, he had done the state a favour and he was the one who had taken all the flak from the Coughlan episode. He was once heard to say, 'I was duped by my police colleagues one night into helping the government out of what could easily have turned out to be a very sticky wicket for them.'

He decided to stay and brazen it out, despite the continued harassment and intimidation by state agents and the threat to his life by the IRA. And he turned out to be right: the committee of inquiry into the cases of arrested and interned civil servants was still considering his application.

They sent the report and remarks on their findings to the minister for finance in May 1931. In their report they stated that what Harling had done for his country during the war of independence was in no doubt, and that his services in the Dáil secretariat then were satisfactory. They also confirmed that the reason for his dismissal from the civil service was that he had taken the side of the Irregular forces in the civil war. They accepted, however, that he had never used his position in the Dáil secretariat to assist the Irregulars. The report concluded, 'The committee are satisfied that he has given up all connection with the Irregular Organisation and that he can be relied on not to again resort to anti-state activities.'

Harling's enemies within the police and government who wanted shot of him were gripped with annoyance when they read the committee's report. They used all the influence they could muster in the Department of Finance to persuade them to ignore the report, but failed. The committee was an independent body outside government control.

On 2 June 1931, the private secretary to the minister for finance received a letter from the executive council telling him that the council had authorised the reinstatement of Seán Harling on the occurrence of a suitable vacancy. Later that month he was reinstated in the paymaster general's office at Oriel House, Dublin – not in his old position as filing clerk, but as a messenger.

He was reluctant to accept the appointment at first, but really had no choice in the matter as, through his own admission, 'during a lengthy period of economic privation I was bordering on starvation'. He said he accepted the appointment under duress and without prejudice to 'my just claim'. He did not give up the fight for reinstatement to his former position.

Chapter 12

Power at Last for de Valera

Just before the general election in 1932 the Cosgrave government banned the annual republican parade to Bodenstown churchyard to honour the memory of the father of republicanism, Theobald Wolfe Tone. Fianna Fáil launched a campaign and organised street demonstrations against the 'undemocratic' banning of the parade, which worked in their favour in the general election.

But during the election campaign supporters of Fianna Fáil and the IRA began attacking and breaking up Fine Gael election rallies. 'No free speech for traitors' was their cry. As a result of those attacks the Army Comrades Association (later to become the Blueshirts) was formed, led by Eoin O'Duffy, to protect the Fine Gael meetings. Continued violent clashes marred the election campaign.

> Once I lay on that sod – it lies over Wolfe Tone –
> And thought how he perished in prison alone,
> His friends unavenged and his country unfreed.
> 'Oh, bitter,' I said, 'is the patriot's meed.'
>
> – *Tone's Grave* by Thomas Davis

The IRA, just like they had done back in the 1918 general election for de Valera and Sinn Féin, worked very hard canvassing for de Valera and Fianna Fáil. After the election, Fianna Fáil, with the help of the Labour party, formed the new Free State government.

De Valera became the new leader. Some commentators of the day said that 'de Valera rode to victory on the backs of the IRA'.

When Fianna Fáil assumed power they released all IRA prisoners, abolished the oath of allegiance to the British crown, and carried out a purge of the civil service, the army and the police. They sacked O'Duffy, Neligan and O'Connell and appointed Éamon Broy as head of both the police and the Special Branch in their stead. The Special Branch later became known to republicans as the Broy Harriers and, in later years, just the Harriers.

The Fianna Fáil-led government appointed a committee to investigate the claims of reinstated and victimised civil servants. Harling immediately submitted an application to the secretary – he was sure he would get his job as filing clerk back now that his old boss de Valera was holding the reins – but his application was rejected. They informed him that his case did not come within the terms of reference. When they told him he remarked sourly, 'The terms must be very limited in scope.' It was beginning to look like some Fianna Fáilers had joined forces with their Fine Gael counterparts to form a powerful blackballing committee against him.

By 1932 the Harlings had three children, two girls and a boy, which qualified them for a local-authority house. They received the keys to 112 Newgrange Road, a new housing estate in Cabra, from Dublin Corporation. Harling brought his parents-in-law to live with them. It was a palace compared to the cramped little gate lodge out in Woodpark and they were delighted with it. But they had rent to pay now and Harling more than ever needed his position back as clerk in the civil service.

They were looking forward to a hassle-free fresh start in Newgrange Road but sadly it was not to be. Cruelly, Harling's past followed him there. Some local petty thief recognised him and spread the word that there was a Carey (an informer) living among them. Soon the cry, 'Squealer!' began to echo around the district. Those who chanted it knew nothing about Harling or his past. Their interpretation of a squealer was a general busybody who ran off to tell the police any time he or she saw anyone breaking the law. Harling's children often had stones thrown at them on their way home from school. He endured all this, all the while battling tooth and nail for his position as clerk in the civil service.

Now that Fianna Fáil were finally in control of the entire armoury in the state, it might have been expected that they would give these arms to the IRA. The volunteers of that organisation were on standby, awaiting the order to march into the final battle that would at last bring the republic into being, and willing once again to wade through Irish blood to achieve that goal.

They did not, and the populace who had been holding their breath breathed a huge sigh of relief. Instead, according to republicans, Fianna Fáil turned their backs on the six counties and abandoned the nationalists to endure the unionist-led pogroms against them. (Collins had once pleaded with the anti-Treaty forces during the civil war to deposit their weapons in the national armoury 'to be stored there until they become a majority in the country in which case they will themselves have control over them'.)

Fianna Fáil purged their party of all undesirables – that is, militants – for their services were no longer required now that the party was finally in power. They set about smashing and splintering the IRA, encouraging former comrades to join the Free State army and police or to remain and become spies for them, just as Harling had done. Éamon Broy successfully recruited a good number of Fianna Fáil and IRA members into his new Special Branch. Times and ideals had drastically changed, it seemed, for the one-time staunch defenders of the republic, the Warriors of Destiny.

During their purge of the IRA the government found time, in 1934, to introduce the Military Service Act. All veterans of the war of independence who sought a pension under this act were requested to submit an account of their activities during the 1917–1921 war, backed up by supporting statements from their former officers. All applications had to be submitted no later than 31 December 1935, when they would be investigated by a referee appointed by the minister for defence. The referee was a member of the judiciary and had statutory powers to interview applicants and witnesses under oath and then to submit his findings to the minister.

Some of the applicants, who were issued the military-service certificate entitling them to a pension under the act were also issued 1917–1921 service medals. Seán Harling received both. He was awarded a medal for his active service as officer commanding the Second Battalion, Dublin Brigade, Fianna Éireann.

Officers of various ranks submitted statements supporting Harling's claim for the awards, but the two most significant names supporting his claim were those of General Seán Caffrey – who, it seems, was involved in the abortive rescue of General Seán Mac Eoin from Mountjoy prison – and the man to whom Harling remained loyal all his life, President Éamon de Valera.

A glimmer of hope appeared on the dark horizon for Harling in 1936, when an examination was held for promotion to clerical grade of persons who had, at any time, served as Dáil messengers. He was eligible to sit the exam but, alas, he failed to qualify. The gods certainly seemed to be against the man. He later claimed that he partly expected to be failed anyway.

In the meantime de Valera and Aiken were growing more ruthless in their routing of the IRA, whose chief of staff since 1938 was Seán Russell. On 18 June 1936 they declared the IRA an unlawful organisation and, after being returned to office in the 1937 general election, de Valera outlawed the Bodenstown commemoration parade. He abolished the Public Safety Act and replaced it with the Offences Against the State Act, and introduced military tribunals and internment without trial.

Fianna Fáil used the Free State army to enforce their new laws and used every means at their disposal to destroy the IRA – including many a new Seán Harling. Many *agents provocateurs* betrayed arms dumps and men to the new Specials.

And those IRA men who joined the Broy Harriers knew only too well what fate lay in store for them if they dropped their guard. They knew that their former comrades would be under orders to get them, so they hounded and harassed and dealt more harshly, viciously and enthusiastically with their former comrades even than the original Free State Specials. It was not uncommon for the Broy Harriers to gun down their former companions when they were resisting arrest.

It was now dawning on those republicans who had withheld judgement on de Valera that he really had abandoned the nationalists in the six counties altogether and that Fianna Fáil had become the real Free Staters.

Take it down from the mast Irish traitors,
It's the flag we republicans claim.
It can never belong to Free Staters,
For you've brought on it nothing but shame.

– *Take It Down from the Mast* by Dominic Behan

Some people were asking what the bloody and savage civil war had been fought for. Others wanted to know what had happened to de Valera's fine election speeches like the one he made on 29 June 1927 at a Fianna Fáil rally in County Clare. There he had instilled in the minds of his constituents his unwavering republican principles, leading them to understand that he would never turn his back on the republic: 'I stand for an Irish republic, for the full freedom of Ireland, as thoroughly today as I stood nine years ago when I first came before you.'

One IRA volunteer who joined the Free State Broy Harriers was Dinny O'Brien, who had fought in 1916 at only seventeen years of age and had later taken part in the war of independence and the civil war on the republican side. He was reputed to have gunned down a number of IRA volunteers, two of them being Liam Rice and Charlie McGlade, while they resisted arrest. Detective Sergeant Dinny O'Brien was himself ambushed and shot dead in his own driveway on Wednesday, 9 September 1942 by four volunteers.

Volunteer Charlie Kerins from Kerry was arrested after half a thumbprint, allegedly his, was found on the handlebars of a bicycle found near the scene. He was tried and convicted of the murder of Dinny O'Brien. Despite the flimsy evidence of the half-thumbprint and the fact that he was not recognised by a group of witnesses for the prosecution who had seen the four men near the scene of the murder, Kerins was sentenced to death by hanging. After Kerins' defence lawyer, Seán MacBride, had failed to convince the court at the appeal hearing to overturn the death sentence on the grounds of lack of evidence, Albert Pierrepoint, the infamous English hangman, was brought over to hang Volunteer Kerins in Mountjoy jail on 1 December 1944.

The relentless hounding of republicans by their former comrades continued into the 1940s and periodic street gun battles took place, mainly in Dublin. While this mini-civil war was going on between the Soldiers of Destiny and their former companions in the IRA, little Seán Harling seemed to have been forgotten about by both sides. He was not punished by Fianna Fáil for the killing of Volunteer Timothy Coughlan, as Seán MacEntee had vowed he would be when they came into power. And the IRA, it seems, never tried to assassinate him.

Undeterred by all the strife between the republicans, Harling's fighting spirit never waned. He complained that he was now being victimised by new personnel in the Department of Finance – people who hated his guts. He carried on the fight, hoping all the time that his old boss de Valera would see him right.

In 1940, however, a desperate Seán Harling was forced by circumstances to write a pleading letter to the Executive Council for reinstatement to the position he had occupied under the provisional government in 1922. He outlined what he had already explained to the previous administration, emphasising that his job in the secretariat was indexing and filing all correspondence. His salary then had been three pounds and five shillings per week. Now it was only one pound and eleven shillings per week, plus bonus, and he had his wife, four children and a mother-in-law to keep. His father-in-law had died the year before. Of the last five men in similar circumstances who had been reinstated to their old positions in the civil service, only one, Joe Reilly, had been employed in the first Dáil before him.

Harling wrote to the taoiseach, Éamon de Valera, appealing to him to intervene on his behalf to end this discrimination and to see that justice was done in his case. He gave the taoiseach the names of the last five men to be reinstated in their old positions and informed him that he was now the only member of staff of the first Dáil not to be reinstated in a position at least commensurate to that which he had held before his dismissal in 1922.

He still held out great hope that Dev would somehow find a way to do right by him, but the taoiseach never replied to his letter. Harling, still loyal to his old boss, believed that it was because he did not want to upset the apple cart. He was hated by some very influential people in the Fianna Fáil party. Also, there was still that influential element in Fine Gael that was insisting that Harling had only ever been employed as a messenger in the first Dáil, no matter what evidence to the contrary was presented to them. Both these groups believed that Harling had betrayed them back in the 1920s and appeared to be united in their determination to block him from getting his position as clerk back.

In January 1940 Harling learned the names of his blackballers. They were on both sides of the divide. He was of the firm belief then that he would find no one to help him and was ready to fight on alone when, to his surprise and delight, he found that there were some people who were willing to speak out on his behalf. The last five men to be reinstated to their jobs, for instance, and some other civil servants, both anti- and pro-Treaty, were prepared to back him in his just claim for reinstatement. All expressed their willingness to testify before the Civil Service Commission, which was supposed to be free of government interference, that he had acted in a clerical capacity in Dáil Éireann until the time of the Treaty, and subsequently in the provisional government.

Between January and May 1940, some of them wrote to the commission on his behalf, swearing that they knew him to have been employed as a clerk in the secretariat up until the beginning

of the civil war. Seán Saunders stated how he used to see Seán
Harling doing clerical work in Diarmuid O'Hegarty's office in
the old Dáil, over the Broadway café in O'Connell Street, and
that he knew he had been on a clerical-grade salary.

Seán Caffrey, who had worked as a messenger in the Department of Agriculture in the old Dáil until 1921 and was now a clerk
in the civil service, wrote to the commission telling them that he
was prepared to give evidence on oath in any court or before any
legally appointed tribunal that during his period of services as
messenger, he had seen Harling doing clerical work and that he
knew Harling's pay had been fifty shillings higher than his. He
told them that he could recall that in 1920, when it was deemed
unsafe to have messengers from each department calling to other
departments, Harling had been charged with the responsibility
of finding and fitting out premises suitable to be used as a central
clearing office, where messages could be left and taken away. He
pointed out that it had also been Harling's responsibility to hire,
and, each week, to pay, the man who ran this office.

> I do not think that any fair-minded man could, under any cir-
> cumstances, suggest that responsible work of this nature would
> be entrusted to a messenger, even to-day, not to mention in 1921,
> when men's lives were in danger and the very existence of the
> republic was at stake.
> The man whom Seán Harling put in charge of the Clearing
> office was transferred to the service of the Provisional Govern-
> ment in 1922 as a clerical officer, and is at present a Staff officer
> in the Department of Defence. I am employed as Civil Servant in
> the Government of Éire.
>
> Seán Caffrey

The following are more letters written to the commission on Harling's behalf:

8a, Richmond Avenue,
Fairview,
Dublin.
12th February 1940

This is to certify that Seán was employed in the secretariat Department of Dáil Éireann during the Period in which I acted as assistant to the secretary, Dermot O'Hegarty.

I found him reliable and trustworthy, and most assiduous in the discharge of his duties. These duties consisted of clerical work usually assigned to junior clerks. In addition, owing to limitations imposed by the critical times then existing, he acted as a despatch carrier to the other government Departments. As a matter of fact, he was largely responsible for the organisation of the central bureau for the transmission of inter-Departmental communications. In connection with the office, a dump was established for the secretion of all official papers and other documents relating to army Organisation, and, here Harling's services were required after office hours at least, once a week, for filing and keeping things in order.

I understand that, practically all the Old Dáil Civil Servants have been re-instated in posts commensurate with their services during the Black-and-Tan period, and I have no hesitation, whatever, in recommending him for the position which he seeks.

Éamon Price

87 Dun Ceannt,
Mount Brown,
Dublin.

16th February 1940

To Whom It May Concern.

This is to certify that Seán Harling was recommended by Finance G.H.Q. to act as Special Courier to Mr E. de Valera, (President of the Executive Council) for the period, Dec. 1920 to June 1921. On Mr de Valera's arrest, he (Seán Harling) was a clerical officer in Dáil Éireann-General Secretariat till he was called up for active service in July 1922. He was appointed by me as O/C Dublin Brigade Fianna Éireann, which position he held until his arrest in September. He was employed in a confidential position as clerk, and his services were very satisfactory.

On his being called back to the Dublin Brigade Fianna Éireann, he was suspended from his position as Clerical Officer – due to his not taking the side of the Free State – and has not yet re-gained his Dáil Éireann status.

In view of the re-instatement of all c.o.'s in Government Departments, I am of opinion, that he should be included in that category, and I would strongly recommend his re-instatement.

Mise,
H. C. Mellows (more commonly known as Barney)
(Late A/G. & D/I. Fianna Éireann, G.H.Q.)

The following letter was sent to the taoiseach, Éamon de Valera, on Harling's behalf by former parliamentary secretary James Dolan:

28, Palmerston Gardens,
Rathmines,
Dublin.

29th April 1940

An Taoiseach,
Government Buildings, Dublin.

A duine uasal,

This is to bring under your personal notice the case of Seán Harling, who has applied to be properly established in the Civil Service.

Red Tape, it would appear, has tied up his case and coldly condemned him to the paltry position he now occupies.

I am convinced, however, that immediately the facts, as disclosed in the accompanying File (apart from your own personal knowledge of the case), you will not allow this grave injustice to continue against a man whom you know has given such outstanding service. I am appealing to you for justice.

Seán suffered injustice under our administration, and it was one of the cases I always felt aggrieved over, knowing as I did the magnificent and outstanding quality of service this man gave when all of us fought together.

Mise le meas,
James N. Dolan

But what if de Valera did decide to run the matter past the head of the civil service? Would he have got past Lemass, MacEntee and Aiken (of whom Harling always said, 'He was a cold, ruthless and unforgiving individual')?

Another glimmer of hope appeared briefly on the gloomy horizon for him once again when, in April 1940, the film censor, J. Montgomery, began collecting all the Irish historical films he knew existed to archive them for historical posterity. He collected all but one, a very important one about de Valera's tour of the USA in 1920. No one knew where that film was. They assumed it had been lost and would more than likely never be found.

But when de Valera was told what Montgomery was looking for he remembered having given it to Seán Harling back in 1921 as a souvenir. He instructed M. Ó Muimhneacháin, a departmental secretary, to write to Harling, asking him to return the film. But Ó Muimhneacháin did not write to Harling. Instead he sent a note to the chief clerk, Harling's boss in the paymaster general's office, on 2 May. The note told the chief clerk that Ó Muimhneacháin had been instructed by the taoiseach to request that he be good enough to enquire from 'Mr Seán Harling, a messenger employed in your office, if he is still in possession of a film containing a record of the Taoiseach's tour of the United States in 1920, and if he has [*sic*], to be good enough to return it. If the film is not in his possession he should be asked what became of it.'

Harling was absolutely delighted when he received the request for the film. He could see himself being reinstated to his old position in the civil service upon handing it over. 'I knew Dev wouldn't let me down,' was perhaps the first thought that came to his mind.

A delighted and very optimistic Seán Harling sat down on 6 May and wrote to his boss.

Chief Clerk,

It will afford me great pleasure to comply with An Taoiseach's request re the Film of his tour in the U.S.A. 1920.

As several attempts were made by unauthorised people in the past to secure it for their own personal gain, I wish to be given the opportunity of presenting it personally to him.

Seán Harling

This was not an unreasonable request, one might think.

The chief clerk sent a copy of Harling's letter to the secretary of the Department of the Taoiseach on the same day he received it from Harling.

Three days later, P. Ó Cinnéide from the taoiseach's office replied to the chief clerk stating that it was not 'feasible to arrange for the Taoiseach to see Mr Harling'. He instructed the chief clerk to tell Harling that he could deliver the film to an officer of the Department of the Taoiseach or alternatively he could give it to the chief clerk to deliver. Ó Cinnéide's letter went on, 'I am to request that you will be good enough to inform Mr Harling accordingly and to notify this office of the course which he proposes to take.'

Why could they not bring themselves to correspond directly with the man? And why was it not feasible to arrange for de Valera to see him briefly to receive the precious film personally from him? Who objected to this meeting? It seems that Harling knew who the objectors were. But who told him?

Harling was bitterly disappointed with the reply from the taoiseach's office and that disappointment was compounded when one afternoon a departmental colleague told him that he had heard Michael Collins' brother, who was a temporary clerk in the civil service at the time, had been made permanent by de Valera.

It took a very downcast Seán Harling another five days to decide whether or not to return the film. Then, on 14 May, he made up his mind and wrote a very short letter to the taoiseach:

Éamon De Valera, Esq., T. D.

A Chara,

I am returning the film of your tour in America as requested.
    In view of the circumstances, under which I came by the film, it meant a lot to me but I realise that you have a prior claim.
    I may add that if a favourable opportunity had presented itself, I hoped to present it to your son, Éamon.

Mise, le meas,
Seán Harling

An interview was quickly arranged for Harling with the government secretary, M. Ó Muimhneacháin, in the taoiseach's department, to hand over the film to him. Harling took full advantage of that interview to argue his case for reinstatement as clerk in the Department of Finance. Before handing over the film he extracted a half-hearted commitment from Ó Muimhneacháin to communicate with him further about being appointed clerk.

Ó Muimhneacháin also promised to send him a receipt for the film.

Harling had no sooner left the office when the taoiseach's secretary, P. Ó Cinnéide, gathered up the film and dispatched it off to the film censor, J. Montgomery, with an note stating:

> The Taoiseach considers that it may be worth while adding the film to your collection of Irish historical films but for the present he desires that no action should be taken in regard to it and that you should merely retain it in your custody until he has an opportunity of viewing it.
>
> P. Ó Cinnéide

Nine days later, not having heard from the Executive Council, an anxious Seán Harling wrote to the secretary:

> A Chara,
>
> With reference to my interview on the 14th instant when I was led to understand that I am to receive a further communication regarding my appointment, I would be glad to know whether a decision has yet been reached.
>
> I would also be glad to have the promised receipt for the film which I handed to you for transmission to An Taoiseach.
>
> Mise, le meas,
> Seán Harling

Ó Muimhneacháin replied to Harling on 23 May, immediately on receipt of his letter, telling him that it had not been intimated at the interview that 'you would receive a further communication from this Department regarding your position in the civil service. The question of your regarding in view of your pre-Truce Dáil Service is proper for consideration by the Minister for Finance and representations in regard to that question should be submitted in the normal official way.' Ó Muimhneacháin enclosed the receipt for the film.

Seán Harling's chances of being promoted to clerical grade in the civil service now stood at nil, since the matter was being referred back to the minister for finance, Seán MacEntee, who hated Harling's guts and who, it appeared, was being backed by other influential blackballers in preventing his promotion. Seán Harling was never forgiven by certain individuals. Being suspected of having played for both sides in the post-civil-war feud, he was now being made to pay the price.

The hostility suffered by Harling and his family in Cabra began to diminish in 1941, when word spread throughout the neighbourhood that he was the recipient of a service medal and after short accounts circulated of his activities during the war of independence. Those neighbours who had initially given him the cold shoulder now had a sneaking regard and respect for him.

Some influential Fianna Fáiler, it seems, one day told Harling that he was wasting his time and energy fighting to get his old job back. It just was not going to happen. On the other hand, though, he had nothing to fear from Fianna Fáil members any more. Harling replied, 'That's because they have more important things to attend to now, like the running of the country.'

But those were still very dangerous times for Seán Harling to be openly walking the streets of Dublin without any form of protection. He was still under sentence of death by the IRA and they had no problem assassinating protected policemen at the time. Archie Doyle, Timothy Coughlan's old pal, was still a very active IRA soldier.

In mid-1940, someone in the IRA began leaking vital information to the Harriers. Suspicion fell on lorry driver Michael

Devereaux, quartermaster of the Wexford Brigade. He was executed in September that year by the IRA. The order for the execution was approved by Stephen Hayes, chief of staff and, later, supposed government informer.

But the leaks continued after Devereaux's execution and this time suspicion fell on Hayes himself. He was arrested by the IRA and held for three months before escaping, manacled, on 8 September 1941. Hardly a wet day had passed after his presenting himself to an garda síochána than the police recovered Devereaux's body from under a pile of stones on the slopes of Slievenamon.

George Plant, who had already been tried for and acquitted of Devereaux's murder, and who had been eighteen months in Arbour Hill on other charges, was tried again for the crime under the hastily arranged Emergency Powers Order 1939. This new law meant that the military court was not bound by any rules of evidence if it considered it proper. The right to use statements given to the gardaí as evidence was allowed to the prosecution but denied to the defence.

This time Plant was found guilty of the murder of Michael Devereaux with Stephen Hayes the sole witness against him. He was transferred to Portlaoise prison, where he was executed by firing squad. Shortly after his execution, the IRA, I understand, sent a representative to Michael Devereaux's widow to inform her that they believed her dead husband had been innocent after all.

One of the soldiers selected for George Plant's firing squad, Private Ned Munroe, marksman, refused to participate in his execution. He was court-martialled, sentenced to six months in the glasshouse, then drummed out of the army.

Seán McCaughey, adjutant general of the IRA, who had been in custody since 5 September 1941, was tried in the military

court on 18 September on the charge of the assault and unlawful detention of Stephen Hayes. He was found guilty and sentenced to death for the crime, which only warranted a maximum
prison sentence of three years, even under the Emergency Powers
Order. Only because a group of what could be described today as
'civil libertarian' lawyers, greatly concerned about the integrity of
the justice system, kicked up a stink, was the sentence commuted
to penal servitude for life. McCaughey was sent to Portlaoise
prison to serve out his sentence, and during his four and a half
years there he never once saw the light of day. He died in the
early hours of Saturday 11 May 1946, after twenty-three days on
hunger and thirst strike, demanding justice.

Detention camps were filled to capacity with republican prisoners
and conditions for them were dreadful under Fianna Fáil. In the jails
of Arbour Hill and Mountjoy and in the Curragh internment camp
(where they were often brutalised by their military police guards)
they were allowed to wear their own clothes, which distinguished
them from criminals, but prisoners in Portlaoise were not and they
had a very rough time.

On arrival at Portlaoise, republican prisoners had their clothes
taken away and were handed prison garb, which they refused to
wear, choosing instead to don the very coarse blankets that were
provided. They were severely punished. They were locked away in
solitary confinement, naked and barefoot, twenty-four hours a
day. They were not allowed out to the toilets, except once a week
to take a bath. They were not allowed to exercise or mix with one
another. They were deprived of all visits, books and papers. They
were prepared to miss mass rather than putting on prison clothes
to attend it. And some died on hunger strike.

Censorship was imposed on all newspapers by the de Valera

government when they reported on the ill-treatment of republican prisoners, which continued into the late forties.

This was the same Fianna Fáil who had bayed for Seán Harling's blood in February 1928 and who had supported the death sentence imposed on him by the IRA in 1927 – a sentence that was still apparently hanging over his head – for 'going wrong' and becoming a detective in the Free State police. A good number of those who had branded him traitor and informer and wanted him shot dead for turning his back on the republic had now turned their own backs on the republic, joining the Free State army and the Special Detective Unit of an garda síochána. According to republican ethos, these people too deserved to meet a traitor's fate, because they had followed a leader who had himself 'gone wrong'.

What a strange turn of events. Only a few years earlier the defenders of the republic were being hounded, shot and imprisoned by the pro-Treaty forces; now they were being hounded, shot and imprisoned by anti-Treaty forces. And the one-time chief of staff, Frank Aiken, was now one of the main anti-IRA men in the state.

In March 1948, the newly elected government, led by Fine Gael and propped up by the new republican party, Clann na Poblachta, led by another one-time IRA chief of staff, Seán MacBride, released the remaining nine prisoners from Portlaoise.

Chapter 13

Cosy Little Chats

When Nelson's pillar was blown up in the early hours of 8 March 1966, I was arrested on suspicion of having played a part in it. I was taken to the Bridewell garda station, where I was held and questioned for two days before being released without charge. Of course, I had absolutely nothing to do with it.

About two hours after my release my aunt Nora, Seán Harling's wife, turned up at our house asking how I was after my ordeal. I wasn't home yet, so my mother told her, 'I don't know, Nora. As far as I'm aware he's still in the Bridewell.'

'No he's not, Bridie, he was released a couple of hours ago,' Nora told her. I had gone to O'Connell Street to see Nelson's rubble and then for a drink with my friends before going home. My mother did not ask her how she knew I had been released.

I arrived home later that afternoon and my aunt was still there. I was surprised to see her, since it was unusual for her to pay my mother a visit. After the niceties I asked her why she had really called. She told me my uncle Seán wanted a word with me. I said I would call over to see him in the morning, and Nora left.

When I entered Harling's house, he asked, 'Well, Nulter, did you do it?' [Nulter is a nickname given to the me by my grandfather. Most of my relatives used that name when I was younger.]

'No,' I replied. 'I had nothing to do with it, uncle Seán. You want to have a word with me, I understand?'

'Yes, I do. Come on into the parlour room with me.'

'About what?' I asked as we walked into the parlour.

'About your political activities,' he said.

'What about them?'

'Are you still in the Dublin Brigade?' he asked.

'No, I resigned last year over a dispute I had with two of my superior officers. It was about what I termed "blind" obedience.'

'What do you mean "blind" obedience, Nulter?'

'Following certain dodgy orders without question.'

'Oh, I see what you mean. Who was the OC then?'

'Now, Daddy Seán,' I said, using the nickname I had given Harling in my childhood so as not to confuse him with his son, also called Seán, who was my godfather. 'You don't really expect me to tell you that, do you?'

'Fair enough, Nulter. I was only asking in case I knew him, or of him. But you must be still connected in some way or you wouldn't have been arrested over the pillar?'

'I just know some people who are connected, that's all.'

'And who are they?'

'Now, Daddy Seán, come on!'

'Well, okay, Nulter. But are you not concerned that they might just be using you?'

'No, I am not. But what's your concern?'

'I'm concerned because I know – not meaning you, mind you – how gullible young volunteers can be manipulated by unscrupulous officers.'

'I'm well aware of that, uncle Seán.'

My uncle Seán, I'm sure, was playing his special-detective role. I had a distinct feeling that he was not just asking those questions off his own bat, although I am certain he was concerned for my welfare at the same time. He flatly refused to tell me how he knew I had been released from the Bridewell that day, saying, 'I just heard it on the grapevine, Nulter, that's all.'

He recounted for me that first day, as he did on subsequent days over the next couple of years, eventful days he had experienced: first as a freedom fighter, then during the civil war and finally as a special detective. He told me he had witnessed some brutal incidents in both wars – but in particular the civil war – that had never gone down on paper, and that very prominent people from both sides had been involved in them. However, he never told me what those incidents or who those prominent people were. Also, he said, during his period as a secret agent, some of the same people were involved in sanctioning certain undocumented and, indeed, sometimes unsavoury events. These people, he said, continued to be prominent members of their respective governments for years afterwards. This led me to the conclusion that not all the unsavoury events of the post-civil-war period were spontaneously carried out by rank-and-filers on both sides. Some, it seems, were well planned and given the nod by persons placed higher up.

Apart from what I have already alluded to in previous chapters, the following is an account of my discussion with Seán Harling that day and on subsequent days, as far as I can recollect.

'Did any of them ever tell you anything about me, Nulter, or ask where I was living?' he began.

'Well,' I said, 'nobody ever went out of their way to tell me anything about you, uncle Seán. But they do know where you live. I remember Frank Drivers asking me one night was I related to the Dartry Road Redicans and to you? I told him I was.'

'But did he tell you anything about me?' Harling said, impatient for my answer.

'Yes, he did as a matter of fact. He told me that you were an informer and that you had murdered Timothy Coughlan, a volunteer in the Dublin Brigade, in cold blood. Is that true, uncle Seán?'

'Well, not really, Nulter.'

'What do you mean? What are you trying to tell me?'

'Look, Nulter,' Harling said, gulping, 'first of all I was a special detective in the Free State secret service, not an informer as Fianna Fáil were making me out to be. And Coughlan and another man called Archie Doyle – I'm sure you've heard of him – had been assigned to kill me.'

'That night, uncle Seán?'

'Well, that's the confusing part of it, Nulter.'

'What do you mean? They either tried to kill you or they didn't.'

'Well,' he said, hedging, 'that was a very worrying time for me.'

'Tell me about it,' I said.

Here Harling paused, deep in thought. I could practically hear his mind working. Then, after about thirty seconds, he stood up and said, 'Wait until I make us a cup of tea.' And off he went into the kitchen.

Harling pottered about in the kitchen for several minutes, probably trying to think up a credible answer to my thorny question. He came back with two mugs of tea and, while handing one to me, he looked me straight in the eye and said, 'Yes, they did try to kill me that night. But I got one of them instead – Coughlan.'

Now his body language seemed to tell me a different story. I was aware that some of his contemporaries, on both sides, were still alive and he more than likely did not want to break the fragile consensus they had built up over the past forty years by coming clean.

Then I asked, 'And what about Doyle?'

'He got away,' was Harling's sharp reply.

'But you must have surprised them somehow. A volunteer of Archie Doyle's calibre and renowned bravery wouldn't just run away from what could be described as a relatively minor gun battle?' I suggested.

'Maybe he just got lucky that night, as I did, Nulter.'

Strange answer, I thought.

'I was their target that night, all right,' he went on, 'and I was supposed to be ambling along my merry way, oblivious to what was about to befall me – like Kevin O'Higgins seven months earlier.'

'Did they kill O'Higgins?' I asked excitedly.

'I don't know, Nulter,' he timidly replied. 'The IRA issued a statement at the time denying any involvement in it, but that, of course, was a load of baloney.'

'But as far as I know the IRA always admitted sanctioned operations. They used to boast about their honesty in that respect.'

'Let me tell you, Nulter,' he asserted, 'back in those turbulent times everybody lied when it suited their cause – including myself. And I'm sure you're acquainted with the term "liberty of action".'

There was spontaneous silence for a couple of minutes. Breaking it, I asked, 'If you were so certain it was Doyle who was with Coughlan that night, why wasn't he arrested afterwards?'

'He was taken in but later released because his alibi stood up.'

'Did you know Coughlan before that night?'

'I knew of him but I had never met him.'

'You were aware of his reputation, though?'

'Who wasn't back then? And, as your uncle Tom once said, "Those are the last two guys in the world a man would want coming after him."'

'Speaking of uncle Tom, did he and uncle Jim play a role in this affair?'

'No, Nulter, none whatsoever. They were in the house at the time. They had no idea what was happening outside until I came in, gun in hand, shouting a warning. They had heard the shooting all right and guessed it was me being attacked. Your uncle Jim, God be good to him, threw a bucket of water at me, thinking I was an intruder. I didn't even know your uncle Tom was coming home that weekend.'

'So the Fianna Fáil version of what happened that night is untrue then?' I suggested.

'Yes, absolutely,' he replied firmly.

'Did any of the Redicans give a statement to the police that night?'

'Not to my knowledge, Nulter.'

'Why not?'

'I don't believe the police asked them to,' he answered.

'Strange, don't you think?' I suggested.

'Yes,' was Harling's very short reply.

'Would it be true to say that you knew Coughlan and Doyle would be there that night?' I went on.

'We had been told it was their turn to watch me that night.'

'Who is we?'

'My superiors and I.'

'So you were expecting to see them there when you arrived home?'

'Not necessarily when I arrived home, but I expected to see them somewhere along the route.'

'Did you discuss the possibility of meeting them along the route with your superiors that night? Did you talk about what tactics you should adopt if they attacked you?'

'No, I didn't, Nulter.'

'Were you not afraid that it might be the night, uncle Seán?'

'The night for what?' he asked, looking bewildered.

'The night for your execution,' I replied, hardly believing that he seemed not to understand the question.

'I was a bit nervous all right, Nulter, but I knew there was an undercover party of my police colleagues patrolling the vicinity in a private car. That was the practice when we knew Coughlan and Doyle would be monitoring my movements, for we had positive intelligence that it would be those two who would be sent out to do the job. We were proved right that night.'

'And did your undercover party turn up during the gun battle?'

'No, they didn't.'

'Why not if they were supposed to be out protecting you?'

'Well, eh … I … eh … I think they had gone back to base thinking I had got home safely,' he stammered. 'I don't remember.'

Then, shifting in his chair, Harling leaned towards me, 'I'm not prepared to discuss the whereabouts of my colleagues that night. Just believe me – what I told you is the way it happened.'

I formed the opinion that he was highly annoyed with himself for having told me about the undercover party in the first place, fearing that I might take the inference (the one that was widely believed by republicans) that the police had in fact played a role in Timothy Coughlan's killing that night.

'Why did you do it, uncle Seán?'

'Do what, Nulter?' he retorted.

'Kill Coughlan,' I was going to say, but instead I said, 'Go wrong.'

He gave me what I can only describe as being a strange reason.

'I never went wrong, Nulter,' he said. 'I did what I did for my country and out of loyalty, and I held the same view as some other men – especially one man whom I greatly admired and respected – about saving gullible young boys in the Fianna from being lured into militantism by unscrupulous and evil men. And before you ask, Nulter, yes, a week's wages played a big part in it too. I was very badly off at the time and nobody on our side, as your aunt Nora rightly pointed out to me daily, seemed to give a damn about my dire domestic circumstances then.'

With his polemic in full swing, I never got the chance to butt in and ask Harling who the person he greatly admired was, although he more than likely would not have told me.

The talk, whether by coincidence or not, moved on to de Valera. As I recall, Harling always defended de Valera in argument and insisted that he was not a man of violence. On the contrary, he abhorred violence, but was never found wanting when he 'deemed it necessary that certain men of violence within our own ranks be rooted out and dealt with'.

'De Valera wanted you dealt with?' I suggested.

'No, he had nothing to do with ordering my execution, Nulter. It was Aiken, I believe, having been chief of staff of the IRA barely a year before, and Russell that pushed for the death sentence to be passed on me.' He added, 'They sent the best they had after me,' and then, after a pause, 'I served my country and Dev well, Nulter. I was always loyal to him and true to the republic.' I wondered whether he was trying to tell me something indirectly.

When Harling told me that de Valera had been dead set against any war with the provisional government forces I smiled cynically, thinking of the speech where he had talked of wading through Irish blood. I asked my uncle, 'Why did he side with the Irregulars in the civil war then?'

'Because he was caught off guard when the Four Courts was shelled,' he answered, gesticulating with his hands.

'What do you mean, off guard?'

'Look,' he said. I sensed a little annoyance creeping into his voice, and guessed it was because he had walked himself into having to explain. 'What I mean is that he was not prepared when it all happened. He didn't want anything like that to happen and he spent all of his time with the Irregulars trying to get them to talk about peace with the Staters. But he only succeeded after Liam Lynch was killed, and that's all I can tell you about that.' Then, in afterthought, he said, 'But I do know that the Irregulars needed Dev. The Staters needed him too. The country needed him.'

I did not bother asking him to explain what he meant by that statement, but I remember wondering whether he was somehow apologising for de Valera's having sided with the Irregulars or whether he was trying to tell me that de Valera only stayed with them to try and persuade them eventually to accept the Free State Dáil as the legitimate seat of authority in Ireland.

Believing I had Harling on a roll, I asked him another question.

'I assume you were talking about after the civil war when you mentioned a moment ago de Valera rooting men of violence out of "our ranks". Tell me, uncle Seán, were you a double agent?'

'I was suspected in some quarters as having being one, and I have suffered the consequences ever since. I have been ostracised by elements from both sides', was his immediate reply.

'But were you one?'

He looked at me pensively before answering, 'I'm afraid I can't confirm or deny that for you.'

'And why not, uncle Seán?'

'Because there are some very prominent men still alive today on both sides from that period who wouldn't want it to be known either way.'

'Like who, for instance, and why?' I insisted.

'I won't tell you who, but I can tell you partially why. I possess knowledge about certain unpleasant and, of course, undocumented events that took place – events that were sanctioned by these people. That's all I'm going to tell you.'

I did not understand that answer, but I can guess that others – old comrades of those prominent people, also still alive at that time but not privy to the collusion between both sides that Harling seemed to be suggesting took place back in the 1920s – would surely have put some very awkward and embarrassing questions to their prominent comrades if it were revealed that Harling had been a double agent. I do not know, either, why he told me that much when he could have left the matter at 'I can't confirm or deny that'.

I stated firmly to him, 'Daddy Seán, the knowledge you profess to have about these people is knowledge, in my opinion, that only a double agent could possess.'

He did not reply. Then, after a moment of silent reflection, he declared, 'I have resigned myself to the fact, Nulter, that history will do me no favours. I made my bed and I lie in it.'

I asked the next question still trying to deduce whether he had been a double agent.

'Uncle Seán, was there anything you knew about the republican movement that would have been of concern to the state that you didn't tell your superiors in the Specials?'

'Yes, there was, Nulter.'

'And what was that?' I ventured.

'I won't tell you, Nulter,' he politely replied. Did that mean he had indeed played a dual role?

The question of how the two bravest and most experienced IRA assassins could miss, by a mile, their target that night was still bugging me. I was determined to find out, so I said to Harling, 'From what I can gather out of what you have told me about that night, uncle Seán, you seemed to have been prepared for the attack.'

'I was. I was at the ready day and night at that time. Our inside men had warned us that an attack on me was imminent. They even advised that it might be better if I left the country for a while. I told them I was not going to leave my family, that I'd rather stay and take my chances.'

'And they accepted that, uncle Seán?'

'Yes, they did. And they told me that they were prepared to help me alleviate my predicament if I wanted. So I carried on with my duties as a detective officer until that fateful night. You and everyone else know the rest.' I wondered whether we did or not. Then he said, sadly, 'I was duped by them.' I presumed he meant the Specials and the government. 'After all that went wrong for me after that night, they abandoned me.'

After a long period of silence I said, 'Tell me did the government and the Specials rejoice when they heard Coughlan was dead?'

'Well, to be honest with you, they did. But they were not the only ones who did. There were others on the other side who were equally, if not more, delighted to hear it.'

I excitedly asked, 'What others? Are you talking about some Fianna Fáilers, for instance?'

'Yes, some, because …' Here he stalled, realising he was about to put his foot in it. Then, going off the subject again, he said, 'Look, there were unpleasant incidents taking place on a daily basis back then. There were certain people, as I told you earlier, on both sides who connived with one another to sort problems out, and they were forced at times to resort to unsavoury methods to do it. And some of those people are alive today. So that story, for the sake of peace and harmony, is best left untold.'

I was, of course, disappointed with that answer, but seeing the anguished look on Harling's face I did not press the matter.

Then, however, after another bout of spontaneous silence, I decided to have another go at wringing out of him what really happened on that cold Saturday night in January 1928.

'You told me earlier that your superiors in the police had told you they could alleviate your predicament for you if you wanted, isn't that right?'

'Yes,' he croaked.

'And did they that night?'

'What do you mean?'

'I'll be straight with you, Daddy Seán. Did Coughlan and Doyle really ambush you that night, or was it the other way around? That's what I mean. Was Doyle even there? And was Coughlan armed?'

Repressing his annoyance, Harling repeated a couple of earlier answers.

'I told you twice already the truth of what happened that night, and of the collaboration between both sides when it was of mutual benefit to them. The undocumented events of that time are best left back there where they belong, so please don't ask me again.'

I let things cool as we both fell silent, sitting back in our chairs in uneasy meditation. I was trying to figure out what the hell the man was trying to tell me. He, it seemed, was delving deep into the dungeons of his memory, among the dark secrets and images of the unsavoury and undocumented events he had locked there almost forty years earlier – which were now, as a result of my questions, floating freely through the corridors of his conscious mind.

He grew weary of the questioning that first day and asked me if I would mind leaving now, saying he did not want to talk any more. I left the house with the gut feeling that he wanted to be more forthright with me but could not trust me not to run off and tell the world. He was sixty-four years old then.

In the chats we had over the next few years Harling was more forthright with his answers to my thorny questions, but he still would not reveal any of the names of the prominent people, on either side during the post-civil-war feud, who participated in or sanctioned the events he claimed occurred. I had a strong impression that Harling, up until his death in 1977, was still wary of some people, old comrades, in both Fianna Fáil and Fine Gael.

My father told me bits and pieces about the affair down through the years, like how his family had reacted the day Harling revealed to them that he was a state agent, corroborating what my uncle Thomas, his brother, had told me. He advised me to leave well enough alone, but that was more easily said than done.

For as long as I can remember, my sisters, brothers and I watched our uncle Thomas Redican torment Seán Harling every time he visited the Harling household to see his mother. Although I later had an idea, we never knew why. One evening, when Thomas came to pay my father a visit and I happened to be there, I took the opportunity to ask him nervously, 'Uncle Tom, why do you torment Seán Harling every time you visit his house?'

He glanced at my father first, then gave me a long scowling look before reluctantly answering, 'Because, that little bollix got our family into very serious trouble a long time ago.'

I ventured, nervously again, 'How did he do that?'

'He turned his coat, that's how,' he yelped back at me, and then stared at me menacingly.

With my nervousness easing, feigning ignorance, I asked, 'What do you mean "turned his coat", uncle Tom?'

'He joined the Free State secret police and spied on his Fianna mates for them. That's what I mean.'

Feigning ignorance again, I said, 'I heard something about him killing a guy called Coughlan back in the 1920s. Is that true?'

'Oh that,' he replied, shaking his head disgruntledly and looking at my father from under his eyelids. 'I thought that that episode was long forgotten. Didn't you, Paddy?'

'Yes,' replied my father uncomfortably, looking at me with displeasure written all over his face.

I let a few moments lapse before asking, 'Can you tell me anything about the Coughlan episode, uncle Tom?'

'Like what?' he asked gruffly.

'Did uncle Seán shoot him, for instance?'

Thomas looked at my father once again, then gave great thought to the question before answering, 'I don't really remember, Nulter, it was so long ago.'

He was obviously lying, for even though uncle Thomas was then in his late seventies there was nothing wrong with his memory. My father was sitting there, livid, with both elbows on the table, his forehead resting in the palms of his hands. Every now and then he lifted his head to give me the look of an angry bull.

Then, all of a sudden, uncle Thomas blurted out, 'Jaysus, Paddy! Do you remember when the Specials first told Harling who the IRA was sending out to kill him? It fairly put the shits up us. Didn't it, Paddy?'

'Yes,' mumbled my startled father, lifting his head and looking menacingly at me with a corrugated brow. I had obviously awakened a long-forgotten event in my uncle Thomas' memory.

Believing that I had opened him up, I rather cleverly got him to tell me something about the whole affair. I asked, hoping that he would not realise I had some knowledge of the event, 'Did you or uncle Jim or any other member of the family play any part in Coughlan's death?'

'Definitely not,' he barked. Then he added, 'But Fianna Fáil at the time tried to make out that I had.'

'Was the account you and uncle Jim gave to the tribunal of what happened that night the true one?' I asked. 'Jesus,' I said to myself, 'I hope he doesn't catch on that I know more than I'm letting on.'

'Yes, it was, Nulter, as far as we were concerned anyway. When Harling walked through the kitchen door with his gun in his hand we really thought the house was under attack. But we later learned that the tale your uncle Seán related to us about the attack on him might not have been wholly true. Didn't we, Paddy?'

My father just nodded his head.

'And what was that, uncle Tom?' I ventured, half knowing that he was not going to tell me.

'That part of the story is best left untold,' he answered with a dismissive wave of the hand.

He was becoming reluctant to talk any more about it. But after some gentle coaxing, he relented.

'Why did the Specials want Coughlan and Doyle out of the way, uncle Tom?' I asked. The moment the words left my mouth I realised my mistake.

'I didn't mention any Doyle during this conversation, did I, Paddy?' said Thomas, turning to my father, who grunted, 'No,' without lifting his head out of his hands. Turning back to me, Tom said, 'Now, I hope you're not acting the bollix with me, for you seem to know more about this business than you're letting on. However, to answer your question, I don't know. I have a good idea, but I'm not going to tell you what it is, except that the Specials weren't the only ones that wanted those two out of their hair.'

'What do you mean, uncle Tom?'

'There were others, supposed enemies of the state, who were even more delighted with Coughlan's killing.'

'Like who for instance?'

'Their names won't cross my lips. I can tell you that they were a pain in their arses with their swashbuckling around the town.'

'Can't you just at least give me a hint as to their identity, uncle Tom?'

'No, I can't,' he snapped, as if angry with himself for telling too much already. Then he meditatively added, 'It doesn't matter now. It was a long time ago and it's best forgotten.'

But I was not satisfied with that. I believed that I was entitled to know the truth of what happened that night. After all, it was part of my family history, albeit a shady part.

'Was Coughlan deliberately ambushed and cold-bloodedly murdered by the police? Was Doyle even there that night? Yes or no?' I demanded.

'I already told you,' said Thomas, getting really riled now. 'I don't know who killed the fucker.'

This is it, I decided now. In for a penny, in for a pound.

'I'm sorry uncle Tom, but I find that hard to believe.'

He flew into a rage, jumped up off the chair and pointed a very menacing finger at me. 'I don't give a curse what you find hard to believe!' he yelled. 'I told you what bloody well happened that night and I'm saying no more. So don't you bloody well ask me again. Do you understand?'

I understood that my uncle Thomas was not a man to be antagonised, even though he was nearly eighty years of age, so I promptly left the subject alone, as my father had earlier advised me to do.

Needless to say, my father gave me a severe telling-off about bringing up those events after my angry uncle Thomas had left the house in a huff. But at a later date, not long before he died, my uncle Thomas opened up and told me a lot more about what he understood might have really happened outside their tiny gate lodge on that cold January night all those years ago.

There were two main conjectures in circulation at the time about Coughlan's killing. One was from Fianna Fáil, which I have already outlined. The other, put about by some state agents, maintained that Coughlan's alleged accomplice, Archie Doyle, accidentally struck Coughlan in the back of the head while firing at Harling. Then, realising what he had done, he panicked and quickly ran away. According to this version of events, Doyle was the mysterious man in the black coat.

But from reading between the lines of what my father and my two uncles had told me about the incident, I have deduced that the Fianna Fáil version of what happened that night – minus the participation of the Redicans – could well be the true one.

As much as they would have liked to, Fianna Fáil did not want to be seen to be directly accusing the Specials – a force they hoped to be in control of in the very near future – as being the perpetrators of the killing, although they did accuse them of covering it up. They had let their true feelings slip at the tribunal of inquiry, when their barristers implied that the gun and Fianna Fáil membership card found on Coughlan's person had been planted there by the police. Instead, they accused the Redicans of colluding with Seán Harling to kill Timothy Coughlan.

There are problems with this hypothesis. The Redicans would have had the courage to carry out the killing, but were they capable of such sophistication? I think not, for to put such an elaborate plan together would surely have taken even the most professional of men four to five weeks, if not longer, especially if they were planning to make the killing look like self-defence. Even if the Redicans had had the acumen to prepare such a plan and had decided to take out the two most feared gunmen in the IRA, they would surely have needed advance knowledge that their targets would be there that night in order to give notice to Thomas Redican in the Curragh to apply for leave to be there that night. Who would have supplied them with that advance knowledge? One of only two groups, in my opinion – the Specials and the IRA themselves.

But despite the story put about by Fianna Fáil of their involvement in Coughlan's killing, the Redicans were never targeted by the IRA because the IRA believed that they had not been involved. James Redican had attended Coughlan's interment in Glasnevin and not one republican there had challenged him. True, they gave evidence at the tribunal of inquiry supporting Harling's version of the event even though they had not witnessed the alleged attack. But they had heard the shots and believed that the house was under attack, especially when Harling appeared at the kitchen door seeming to confirm that opinion. Harling knew that he would get full cooperation from the Redicans if he could persuade them that IRA volunteers were attacking their home. That is why they backed Harling's version of events at the tribunal of inquiry. But the Redicans later heard a different version of what could well have been the true events of that night.

The news of the killing of Volunteer Timothy Coughlan and

the lucky escape of Volunteer Archie Doyle sent shock waves through the ranks of Fianna Fáil, as I believe it was designed to do. But who selected those two for assassination – that is, if it was a political assassination – and why? Were they considered a potential embarrassment to Fianna Fáil by some of the members, who skulked in the background with their Free State counterparts discussing what should be done about them?

Harling would have us believe that the police knew that Coughlan and, allegedly, Archie Doyle were to be sent out to Woodpark that Saturday night on a mission to kill him. So instead of a plot to ambush and kill Timothy Coughlan and the alleged Archie Doyle being hatched in the Redican household, could it have been hatched in Dublin Castle, or indeed in Pearse Street garda station?

According to Harling, 'certain garda operations went unrecorded'. It is known that a lot of very unsavoury methods were used by the police when trying to extract information from republican prisoners, such as vicious beatings and torture. And two of Harling's superiors, Superintendent Ennis and Inspector Kinsella, who had arrested and been put in charge of the prosecution of the ten IRA officers accused of conspiring to murder Kevin O'Higgins, were accused of participating in that beating and torture.

It was well known, too, by republicans that Harling's immediate superior, Superintendent Finian O'Driscoll, was a vicious and nasty man. It is documented that O'Driscoll and another CID detective named Finian Hartigan went down to Waterford to interrogate a prisoner, William O'Donoghue of Cappagh, County Waterford, in November 1926. On 23 November they took him out the Dungarvan Road in a car, where they beat and tortured him. An inquiry into the incident was held in Cappoquin, County Waterford and it was found that the two detectives had indeed assaulted O'Donoghue. He was awarded compensation.

It is historically known, furthermore, that after the assassination of Kevin O'Higgins, the government feared that the IRA were planning more assassinations of ministers. Harling told me that 'the government and the Specials wanted retribution as quickly as possible'. It is true to say that the Specials did not know who had killed O'Higgins, but they had their suspicions. According to Harling they bandied about a couple of names of who they thought could be the culprits. And they vowed to take revenge. Some of them, encouraged by O'Duffy, wanted to go out and take revenge almost immediately. O'Duffy declared, 'We should take out their hardest.'

But if elements in the Specials wanted rid of Coughlan and his accomplice, if for no other reason than the fact that they were considered the hardest gunmen in the Dublin Brigade, they could not be seen to pull the trigger themselves.

We know that Fianna Fáil and the IRA, after months of watching Harling's movements, would have been well acquainted with his routine. Therefore they would have planned their attack on him around that routine. The two volunteers sent out to do the job would more than likely have secreted themselves in the grounds of Woodpark, or in any of the secluded residences beside it, which would have supplied ample cover for their ambush. It was much less likely that they would have positioned themselves, as stated at the tribunal of inquiry, on the far side of the road.

Though great stress was laid on this circumstance at the time, we should not forget that Coughlan and Doyle were two of the men that had gunned down the Free State minister for justice only six months earlier, in broad daylight and in front of dozens of witnesses. That fact was not known then, however, having only been revealed since in Vincent McEoin's book, *Harry: The Story of Harry White* (1985).

Seán Harling alleged that the Specials were planning to take revenge for the killing of Kevin O'Higgins. Let us suppose that they saw the night of 28 January 1928 as a golden opportunity to exact that revenge. They could stage the whole show without fear of being seen to be the perpetrators. It was well and widely known that Fianna Fáil and the IRA wanted Harling shot dead. Indeed, they were determined to see that it was done professionally by sending out their very best to do it – and it was those very best that the Specials wanted off the scene permanently. Who would not have believed, besides Fianna Fáil of course, that Harling had killed two of their volunteers in self-defence?

Let us suppose that Harling's superiors had him sufficiently terrified and convinced at work that Saturday afternoon that they had received copper-fastened information that morning that an attempt on his life at the hands of Coughlan and Doyle was to take place that very night. Let us suppose, then, that they told him that they could and were willing to solve the problem for him – but only at a price and with his full cooperation.

Let us also suppose that the official police car, which Harling admitted he had got a lift in that night as far as the corner of Kenilworth Square was, in fact, the private car he had talked about, and that it contained five persons, not just three as stated at the tribunal of inquiry. Let us suppose it was driven by its detective owner, and that it did not make any stops along the route, but instead drove straight to Woodpark lodge. We must bear in mind that not one of the witnesses called by counsel for the police at the tribunal of inquiry mentioned seeing Harling, or any other man, walking along that side of the road on that fateful night.

The car, then, would have arrived much earlier than stated. The five men would have alighted and concealed themselves either in St Kevin's Park or in the grounds of the house called Ard-na-Cree, opposite Woodpark and behind the seat on which Fianna Fáil alleged Coughlan eventually met his doom, to await the coming of Coughlan and Doyle.

Let us suppose now that Doyle did not turn up that night and that Coughlan was there alone and unarmed, sitting on the bench opposite Woodpark, enjoying a smoke while waiting to check the time at which Harling arrived home, when he was bushwhacked and shot through the back of the head. Let us suppose that his assailants then carried him into the grounds of Woodpark, then staged a mock attack on the house.

And what about the two men allegedly seen getting off the tram at the corner of Woodpark and stopping to have a chat beside a private car opposite Woodpark lodge, completely unperturbed while bullets whizzed about them? Were they members of the Special Detective Branch who had arrived in the very car they were standing beside, not by tram at all?

We might also suppose that the panic-stricken man dressed in black seen running from the direction of Woodpark with bullets flying after him was in fact a terrified innocent passer-by who, frightened for his life, bolted in panic up Orwell Park. This would have turned out to be a blessing in disguise for the Specials, who would have used it to lend credence to their cover story. David Neligan derived great pleasure out of telling how the man in the black coat (meaning, though never explicitly mentioning,

Archie Doyle) would have won a gold medal in the Olympic games that year with the speed he ran away from the gun battle. How did Neligan know this? Was he present at the gun battle? Did he see a man running for his life?

And when the shooting was all over, the two men standing at the car, who had paid no attention either to the bullets flying all around them or to the panic-stricken man running past them, would have jumped on a tram heading back to town. All the other detectives would have piled into the private car they had come in and driven off, leaving Harling to recite to his in-laws and to the local police the prepared story.

We might even dare suppose that Volunteer Timothy Coughlan was shot through the back of the head not by a bullet fired from Seán Harling's gun, but by one fired from the weapon of a police colleague, with Harling's agreement to take the fall for it.

The above-outlined scenario, if true, would have been orchestrated by the Specials to send a specific and clear message to Fianna Fáil and the IRA: an eye for an eye and a tooth for a tooth. At the same time it would have sent a sinister warning to Archie Doyle that he was next on their hit list. And after all, it is not altogether unbelievable. Harling once told me that General O'Duffy sought permission from the government to wipe out the whole Dublin Brigade of the IRA, but was refused.

Epilogue

Fianna Éireann did not split when Sinn Féin and the IRA did after the Dáil vote on the Treaty, but the vast majority of them took the side of the Irregulars in the civil war. Seán Harling was one of them and was suspended from his job as a filing clerk in the Dáil secretariat because of it, which was understandable under the circumstances.

But by the time Harling was released from prison in February 1924, the Fianna had already passed a resolution renouncing militancy and announced their intention of becoming strictly a national boy-scout organisation. Before his release he signed the declaration of fidelity and announced his support for the non-militant faction in the Fianna.

So, after it renounced militancy and became strictly a scouting organisation, should Seán Harling's membership of the Fianna have legally prevented him from returning to his civil-service post? The Clann na nGaedheal-led government was still suspicious of the Fianna (the majority of them were still anti-Treaty) and suspended Harling indefinitely because of his continued association with that organisation. But at the tribunal of inquiry into Timothy Coughlan's death, counsels for an garda síochána and Seán Harling alluded to the fact that members of Fianna Éireann, a group that never split, were free to join other organisations and still be members of the Fianna. Was not the state, then, acting illegally by barring Harling from his civil-service post? And later, did not the Fianna Fáil-led government also act illegally by denying him clerical status in the civil service?

Why Seán Harling joined the Free State secret service is a question to which we will never know the answer. He himself never told a single soul categorically why he did it. He gave interviews to several individuals during the 1960s and gave to two of those people, I understand, two different reasons as to why he did it? None of them true of course. The main conjecture at the time, which remains to this day, was that poverty was the main reason. This could well be true, because according to the story told in this work the Specials drove Harling to poverty with the purpose of forcing him to work for them. And David Neligan, Harling's handler, often almost boastingly, stated that poverty had driven Harling to work for the state. He never mentioned the psychological torture and heavy intimidation he and his men first meted out to Harling.

But I believe, although I cannot prove it, that with the encouragement of one or more anti-Treaty republicans Harling joined the Specials to become a double agent. I believe that he also had a republican handler, although again I have no proof of this.

Another belief of mine is that Harling's cover as a state agent might never have been blown if it were not for the stupidity of the Specials in arresting Volunteer Healy, a minor player in the overall scheme of things, and sending him to jail over a very small quantity of old arms and ammunition. This came at the start of Harling's spying career, and quickly put an end to his work in the Fianna for the Specials. It also put his life in jeopardy.

I often wonder whether, if Fianna Fáil had been able to form an administration in 1927, they would have called off the assassination order on Seán Harling? Would their minister for justice have retained him as a special intelligence officer in an garda síochána? Or would they have carried out MacEntee's vow of vengeance?

Also, I cannot help but wonder whether Harling was ever really a target for the IRA? After all, he openly walked the streets of Dublin, especially when he returned from Canada, unarmed and totally unprotected at a time when the IRA were supposed to have ordered their liberty-of-action men to take him out. This was a time when the IRA were gunning down policemen, like Sergeant Dinny O'Brien, and other well-protected targets. If I believe that Harling had a republican handler then I must also believe that that handler was protecting his life.

Another abiding question is why de Valera, the man Harling said he remained loyal to all his life, remained silent and tight-lipped throughout Harling's long post-civil-war battle to win recognition from both the Fine Gael- and Fianna Fáil-led governments as having been a clerk in the first Dáil.

Out of all the republicans who 'went wrong', Harling was the most hated and vilified, and the only one of them who survived into old age to lose out seriously. He remained the victim of a lingering hatred (acquiring the nickname Leather Lips), but all in all his former comrades seem to have left him in peace to live out a normal life. And until his dying day, whenever the Cough-lan affair came up for discussion, he stuck to the story of two assassins. What I have discovered during this short stroll through republican history is how a volunteer who falls out of favour with his compatriots can so easily be airbrushed out of their history. But I ponder, since Harling told me that, 'I did what I did for my country', did he give up his life for Ireland without having actually physically died for her?

I do not know whether the bank raids carried out by Commandant James Redican and his crew were official or unofficial, but it is true that he, shortly after his release from prison, claimed he could produce evidence to prove that they had been officially sanctioned by the IRA and the names of those who had participated in the raids with him. No evidence, however, was produced or asked for. Neither was any evidence produced to the contrary, save for the findings of the Court of Conscience. James Redican was adamant that he had handed over the proceeds of the raids to his immediate superior officer, Brigadier Burke, commander of the South Westmeath Brigade. Burke, for some unknown reason, kept silent on the matter.

Was Redican hinting that some high-ranking IRA officer or officers had siphoned off the money for himself or themselves after he had handed it over, then stitched him up? If it was true that Redican and his crew never counted the proceeds from the raids, how would they or the IRA high command know whether the money had gone missing before or after being handed over to Redican's superior officer in Mullingar? The IRA army council claimed that they had never received a single penny from the bank raids and that they had no knowledge of the raids until they heard about them at the court martial.

When the IRA saw that Redican had employed counsel to defend him at the court martial they believed that he was recognising the authority of a British court in Ireland, and disowned him. At that time, however, volunteers who were brought to trial and faced the death sentence if found guilty could hire counsel to defend themselves. James Redican, besides the charge of raiding the bank, had two charges against him. The more serious was that of shooting at the Auxiliaries with intent to murder, which carried a possible death sentence.

Volunteers were automatically disowned by the IRA when charged with a criminal offence, but, depending on the circumstances, they could later sanction the operation involved, a tradition within the republican movement which exists to this very day.

The British knew that James Redican and his men were IRA activists and must have believed that the bank raids were IRA sanctioned – otherwise they would have been tried in Green Street criminal courthouse (which was where serious criminal offences were usually tried) instead of in Kilmainham and Richmond barracks by British field general court martial. Had they been tried in Green Street the charges against them would more than likely have been dropped for lack of evidence.

Three months had passed, and the civil war had been raging for two of those months, since the Redican brothers had appeared at the Court of Conscience in South William Street, Dublin. In the meantime, the two judges that presided had split, Arthur Clery going with the Irregulars and Creed Meredith siding with the state. Only then did Ernest Blythe, acting minister for home affairs, send the directive of their findings to the governor of Mountjoy to read to the Redicans. The directive, of course, stated that neither judge had found that a miscarriage of justice had taken place in their case.

I am not suggesting that there was anything sinister behind Ernest Blythe's delay in sending out the findings of the two judges. When the directive did arrive, however, James Redican challenged that version as being incorrect, arguing that the hearing never reached a conclusion because the bombardment of the Four Courts had begun. He believed that Arthur Clery had recommended their release. Could he have been right?

Timothy Coughlan and Archie Doyle were two of the most dedicated volunteers to the cause of the Irish republic. When ordered to carry out a mission they did so without question and with enthusiasm, professionalism and bravery. They allowed nothing and nobody to deter them in their effort to carry out their mission successfully. Their unquestionable loyalty and dedication to the cause drew admiration and appreciation from most of the high-ranking members of the Fianna Fáil party. But those high-ranking members of Fianna Fáil, four years later, went on to betray them.

If Archie Doyle's name was bandied about during the Coughlan affair with the intention, as was suggested, to scare him away from militant activity against the state, then it failed. Archie Doyle went on to become more active in the IRA than ever. He rose in rank to become quartermaster general and was a member of the general headquarters staff. I met and spoke to Archie Doyle on a few occasions during the late 1960s and early 1970s. He died an unrepentant soldier of the Irish republic in St James' hospital, Dublin, in 1980.

Although it is widely believed today that Timothy Coughlan, Archie Doyle and Bill Gannon, a supposed member of Michael Collins' Squad (and all members of Fianna Fáil at the time), were the assassins of Kevin O'Higgins, I have no way of knowing if this is true. It is also rumoured that Archie Doyle danced for joy on the grave of Kevin O'Higgins, but this may be false.

Timothy Coughlan, it is said, was only fifteen years of age when he fought against the Black and Tans and seventeen years of age when he fought on the anti-treaty side in the civil war. He was captured and interned for most of the civil war and for a short period afterwards. Shortly after his release from prison, and while still a member of Fianna Éireann, he joined the Dublin Brigade of the IRA and subsequently Fianna Fáil. He was twenty-three years of age, the second eldest of nine children, and had been working as a builder's labourer in Drumcondra at the time of his killing.

I find it hard to believe that Seán Harling's and Timothy Coughlan's paths never crossed, even though they were both members of the Dublin Brigade of Fianna Éireann and were both interned around the same time. But denying knowing Timothy Coughlan, from my research anyway, seems to have been a favourite diversion of that time. Anyone questioned about him before and during the tribunal of inquiry denied knowing him, including Joseph Reynolds, who left the Fianna at the same time as Coughlan to join Fianna Fáil.

My aunt Nora told me that Seán Harling finally regained his long-fought-for position as clerk in the civil service in 1941 – thanks, I am led to understand, to having returned that precious film of Éamon de Valera's tour of the USA. He retired in 1966 on a small pension and started a sweet factory in the big garage at the back of his house to supplement his income.

All veterans of the war of independence who were alive on 11 July 1971 and who had been awarded the 1917–1921 service medal received the newly created jubilee anniversary of the truce medal, known as the truce commemoration medal. Seán Harling, of course, was awarded one. He died six years later, on 20 August 1977, after suffering a heart attack. He is buried in St Paul's cemetery, Glasnevin, Dublin, in the grave he had commandeered and in which he had buried the young Fianna Éireann volunteer William Clarke fifty-five years earlier. Members of the government and the civil service sent messages of condolence to his widow. A number of them and other dignitaries attended the funeral.

The following is how Harling's passing was reported in the *Irish Press* and the *Irish Independent* on 24 August 1977:

A former Brigadier General of Fianna Éireann, Mr Seán Harling, who became the first A.D.C. to the late President de Valera, has died in the James Connolly Memorial Hospital in Dublin, aged 75.

Mr Harling, who spent most of his working life as a clerical officer in the Department of Finance and who was a native of Dublin, was buried in Glasnevin Cemetery yesterday. Military honours were rendered by an army firing party and a guard of honour of Fianna veterans under Mr Christopher Doyle was also present.

James Redican, having found work and marrying in 'the land of the auld enemy', was killed in Camden town, London, in the summer of 1940 along with his wife and one of their four children. A German bomber, in one of the first daylight bombing raids on London, landed a direct hit on the air-raid shelter in which the family had taken refuge. Redican's other three children survived the bomb and were sent back to Dublin to be reared by the Harlings in Cabra, where one of them died of a fever shortly after arriving.

Thomas Redican worked as a bus driver for a couple of years having come out of the Free State army. He spent the rest of his working life as a customs officer in the Dublin docks. He died of natural causes in May 1978 and was buried with military honours.

His sister Nora Harling died, also of natural causes, on 8 June 1983 and is buried with her husband in St Paul's, Glasnevin. Redican's younger brother, Patrick, had been a drummer in the Irish Citizen Army pipe band. I was told that he belonged to a small group of young men, not members of the republican movement, who worked with a Fianna Éireann unit from Rathmines, under the command of Christy Doyle, on certain covert operations. I was told by Christy Doyle that Patrick Redican had been Countess Markievicz' secret courier but I cannot prove this. He died of natural causes in 1986 and he, too, was buried with military honours.

Éamon de Valera, Frank Aiken, Seán Lemass and Seán MacEntee became well-known and respected national and international statesmen and could well be responsible for laying the foundation stone for the economical miracle that is Ireland today. They were, however, one-time revolutionaries, and revolutionaries throughout the world, no matter what their cause, do and say things that they would not dream of during times of peace and freedom.

All antagonists concerned with this story are now dead.

Finally, my own memories of Seán Harling are of a strongwilled but kind and gentle soul:

> I passed on my way, God be praised that I met her.
> Be life long or short, sure I'll never forget her.
> We may have brave men but we'll never have better.
> Glory-O! Glory-O! To the bold Fenian men.

> – *Down by the Glenside (The Bold Fenian Men)*
> by Peadar Kearney

Acknowledgements

My thanks to David Craig, Director of the National Archives, and to Aideen Ireland, senior archivist for giving me permission to use the information I obtained from the archives – document reference NAI, D/Taoiseach No. S. 5598 is the transcript from the Tribunal of Inquiry into the Death of Timothy Coughlan at Woodpark Estate on the Dartry Road on 28 January 1928. It commenced its Public Hearing on 27 February 1928. Likewise document reference No. S. 5069 contains letters written by Seán Harling to the Committee of Inquiry into Dismissed Civil Servants and their replies and some letters from Harling to different government departments about his case from 1926 to 1940. Also the Penal Servitude File NAI [Penal Servitude File, 49/50], which consists mainly of petitions by James Redican (document reference No. E. 571) to the Prisons Board Authority and petitions written on his and his brother Tom's behalf by the prison chaplain from March 1922 until their release on 2 July 1924 (document reference No. E. 572). I also extend my thanks to the other archivists and general staff for their courtesy and help with my research especially Gregory O'Connor, who over some weeks, spent what seemed like hours down in the bowels of the archives (and at a time when the building was undergoing extensive renovations) retrieving very important information for me that proved invaluable for the completion of this book. Thank you, Gregory.

My thanks to Margaret Kilcommins and the Department of Defence, Financial Branch, for supplying me with the official details of Seán Harling's War of Independence Service record and for granting me permission to use same in this work.

I wish to acknowledge the National Library of Ireland, Kildare Street, Dublin, and the research Department of Pearse Street Library,

Dublin, and their staff for helping me scan through newspapers from the period held in their possession.

I am grateful to Rena Dardis and Anvil Books for kindly giving me permission to quote some material from Terence de Vere White's excellent book, *Kevin O'Higgins*.

I want my family and good friends to know that I dearly appreciate the support and encouragement they gave me to finish this work.

And my very special thanks to Mercier Press for agreeing to publish this story and for their very expert advice on how to properly structure my work. I am indebted to them and will be forever grateful to them.

THE

SQUAD

and the

intelligence operations of

Michael Collins

T. RYLE DWYER